RUSSIAN SOCIAL THOUGHT IN THE 19ᵀᴴ CENTURY

Russian Social Thought in the 19ᵗʰ Century is a comprehensive introduction to pre-Soviet Russian social theory, tracing its evolution through the works of influential thinkers such as Pyotr Chaadaev, Leo Mechnikov, Mikhail Bakunin, Pyotr Kropotkin, and Pavel Lilienfeld. This pioneering text weaves together a chronological narrative that highlights the overlapping contributions of these intellectuals, rediscovering the broader roots of sociology within Russia's rich historical and philosophical landscape. By synthesizing key ideas and movements, the book provides an indispensable foundation for understanding the development of Russian social thought and its enduring impact on global intellectual traditions.

Designed for an academic and scholarly audience, this book is an essential resource for students, educators, and researchers in Russian social theory, philosophy, sociology, history, and political science. It invites readers to delve deeply into the intellectual currents of 19th-century Russia, offering fresh insights and critical perspectives for those seeking to expand their understanding of social theory's historical dimensions.

Ananta Kumar Giri is Founding Honorary Executive Trustee of Vishwaneedam Centre Asian Blossoming, Puducherry and Chennai, and a former Professor at the Madras Institute of Development Studies, Chennai, India. He has taught and done research in many universities in India and abroad. He has an abiding interest in social movements and cultural change, criticism, creativity and contemporary dialectics of transformation, theories of self, culture and society, and creative streams in education, philosophy, and literature. Giri has had an abiding interest in the philosophies and practices of yoga, especially the integral yoga of Sri Aurobindo and the Mother, and he is now cultivating pathways for a new social and planetary yoga. He has written, edited, co-edited, and translated more than six dozen books in Odia and English, including *Global Transformations: Postmodernity and Beyond* (1998); *Knowledge and Human Liberation: Towards Planetary Realizations* (2013); *Bahudhara Barnabiva* (Splendrous Beauty of the Plural, 2021); *The Calling of Global Responsibility: New Initiatives in*

Justice, Dialogues and Planetary Realizations (2023); *Rethinking Satyagraha: Truth, Travel and Translation* (Editor, 2025); *Cultivating Gardens of God: A Paradigm Shift in Faith* (Editor, 2025); *Contemporary Contributions to Critiques of Political Economy* (Editor, Routledge, 2024); *New Works in Consciousness Corridors: Dialogues with Subhash Sharma and Creative Planetary Futures* (Co-editor, Authors Press, 2023); *Rethinking Media Studies: Media, Meditation and Communication* (Co-editor, Routledge, 2024); *Towards a Dharma of Peace Building* (Co-editor, Springer, 2023); *Covid-19 and the Challenges of Trauma and Responsibility* (Co-editor, 2025); *Quest for Planetary Well-Being: Essays in Honor of M V Nadkarni* (Co-editor, 2026); *The Calling of Global Responsibility: New Initiatives in Justice, Dialogues and Planetary Realizations* (2023); *Social Healing* (2023); and *Cultivating Integral Development* (2023).

Artem Uldanov is an assistant professor at Politics and Governance School, HSE University in Moscow, in the Russian Federation. His research is mainly in political science and public policy. He has written on issues of public participation in authoritarian political regimes and the applicability of different public policy theories in an authoritarian institutional landscape. His recent research focuses on policy narratives in Russian context and the comparative analysis of recent mass protests in former Soviet republics.

Sergey Parkhomenko has a PhD in sociology from Moscow State University n.a. M.V. Lomonosov and an MPA from Maxwell School of Citizenship and Public Affairs at Syracuse University, NY, USA. He is an associate professor at Politics and Governance School and the deputy head of the Laboratory for Anti-Corruption Policy at HSE University, Moscow. His main research interests lie in the field of anti-corruption studies, public governance, and public policy. His recent research focuses on the sociology of corruption, anti-corruption education and training, and the implementation of anti-corruption policies in public sector.

Arnab Roy Chowdhury is an associate professor in the School of Sociology at HSE University, Moscow, in the Russian Federation. Prior to this, he was an assistant professor in the Public Policy and Management Group at the Indian Institute of Management, Calcutta (IIMC). His research and teaching interests include sociological theory, forced migration and refugee studies, social movement studies, ethnicity and nationalism, agrarian studies, natural resource extraction and labour, comparative and historical sociology, and postcolonial and subaltern studies.

Deirdre Ruscitti Harshman is an assistant professor in the Department of History at Christopher Newport University, USA, as well as the book review editor of *The Soviet and Post-Soviet Review*. Her research focuses on modern Russian and Soviet history, particularly in conversation with urban studies and the history of everyday life, and she is currently working on a book project entitled "The Unruly Everyday: Managing Housing, Home, and the Russian City, 1890–1935."

RUSSIAN SOCIAL THOUGHT IN THE 19TH CENTURY

Edited by Ananta Kumar Giri, Artem A. Uldanov, Sergey Parkhomenko, Arnab Roy Chowdhury, and Deirdre Ruscitti Harshman

Routledge
Taylor & Francis Group

LONDON AND NEW YORK

Designed cover image: Credit- Photos.com

First published 2026
by Routledge
4 Park Square, Milton Park, Abingdon, Oxon OX14 4RN

and by Routledge
605 Third Avenue, New York, NY 10158

Routledge is an imprint of the Taylor & Francis Group, an informa business

For Product Safety Concerns and Information please contact our EU representative GPSR@taylorandfrancis.com. Taylor & Francis Verlag GmbH, Kaufingerstraße 24, 80331 München, Germany.

Trademark notice: Product or corporate names may be trademarks or registered trademarks, and are used only for identification and explanation without intent to infringe.

British Library Cataloguing-in-Publication Data
A catalogue record for this book is available from the British Library

ISBN: 978-1-032-27126-2 (hbk)
ISBN: 978-1-032-89054-8 (pbk)
ISBN: 978-1-003-54100-4 (ebk)

DOI: 10.4324/9781003541004

Typeset in Sabon
by Deanta Global Publishing Services, Chennai, India

CONTENTS

List of contributors   *vii*

Preface   *xi*

An Introduction and an invitation   1
Ananta Kumar Giri, Artem Uldanov,
Sergey Parkhomenko, Arnab Roy Chowdhury,
and Deirdre Ruscitti Harshman

1   From sociological to geographical thoughts of Lev Ilyich
    Mechnikov: Society and the law of cooperation   9
    Monika Verma

2   Mikhail Aleksandrovich Bakunin: A life of theory,
    a life of praxis   26
    Deirdre Ruscitti Harshman

3   Alexander Stronin: Foundations of Russian
    Political Sociology   41
    Md Reza Habib

4   Pavel Lilienfeld: Common patterns between the nature
    and society   56
    Liudmila Zhdanovich

5 Nikolay Konstantinovich Mikhaylovsky: The Narodnik
   movement—background and critique   70
   Alex Moore

6 The moral doctrine and epistemic sphere of
   Vladimir Solovyov   83
   Feeza Vasudeva

7 The philosophical and sociological views of N. I. Kareyev
   in the context of modern cognitive management   99
   Jacopo Agostini

8 Revisiting the "Positive philosophy" through the life and
   work of Eugène de Roberty: The foundational scholar of
   Franco-Russian sociology in the 19th century   114
   *Ahmed Abidur Razzaque Khan and
   Abdur Razzaque Khan*

Index   *127*

LIST OF CONTRIBUTORS

Jacopo Agostini completed a three-year degree at the University of Padua, Italy, and a double major at EHESS in Paris and HSE in Moscow, all in sociology. He currently contributes to the pages of the newspaper *il manifesto* and the art magazine *Arte e Dossier* and has participated in several humanitarian and environmental projects around the world. His areas of interest include documentary and human photography, the documentation of abandoned places, urban exploration, and the social and cultural narratives found in forgotten and derelict spaces. In his work, he explores the intersection of memory, identity, and the urban environment, highlighting the significance of overlooked landscapes in contemporary society.

Tatiana Chubarova holds a Ph.D. (Social Policy, LSE) and a Doctor of Economics (Russian Academy of Sciences) degrees and is a Senior Research Fellow at the Institute of Economics, Russian Academy of Sciences, Moscow, Russia. She also teaches at the Moscow School of Economics, Lomonosov Moscow State University. Chubarova has contributed as an editor and author to a number of books, such as *Social Policy, Poverty, and Inequality in Central and Eastern Europe and the Former Soviet Union: Agency and Institutions in Flux* (2019) and *Comparative Health Care Federalism* (2015). Recently, she co-authored "Public policy responses to the spread of COVID-19 as a potential factor determining health results: a comparative study of the Czech Republic, the Russian Federation, and the Slovak Republic," *Central European Journal of Public Policy*, Volume 14 (2020): Issue 2, and "International knowledge transfer and Russian social policy: The case of gender mainstreaming," *Global Social Policy*, 2020.

Natalia Grigorieva is a professor of Sociology at the Faculty of Public Administration, Lomonosov Moscow State University (Moscow, Russia). She holds a Doctor of Science Degree in Political Science (MSU) and is the Head of the Centre of Comparative Social Policy and Gender Studies. Her professional interests include comparative social policy, with a special interest in health care policy and gender studies. She is the author (and co-author) of over 150 research monographs, reports, book chapters, articles, and pamphlets. Her recent publications in English include "International knowledge transfer and Russian social policy: The case of gender mainstreaming" (with Tatiana Chubarova), *Global Social Policy*, 2020, November 23; "Equality and inequality in social scientific studies in Russia, 2000–2015" in *Social Policy, Poverty, and Inequality in Central and Eastern Europe and the Former Soviet Union*, 2019; "Social justice and equality/inequality issues" in The World Social Science Report 2016, UNESCO.

Md Reza Habib is an Assistant Professor in the Department of Social Sciences and Humanities at Independent University, Bangladesh (IUB). He holds a Ph.D. in Sociology from HSE University, Moscow, Russia. He earned his bachelor's, master's, and M.Phil. degrees in Anthropology from the University of Dhaka, Bangladesh, and completed a second master's in Population and Development at HSE University, Russia, in 2019. His research interests include migration, refugee studies, community media, gender, and public health. He has published several double-blind, peer-reviewed articles in reputable academic journals and presented his work at various international conferences. In addition to his academic work, he has received professional training in project management and research methodology through workshops and seminars both nationally and internationally. He has also worked with organizations such as InM, ICDDR, B, and RTM International.

Deirdre Ruscitti Harshman is an assistant professor in the Department of History at Christopher Newport University, USA, as well as the book review editor of *The Soviet and Post-Soviet Review*. Her research focuses on modern Russian and Soviet history, particularly in conversation with urban studies and the history of everyday life, and she is currently working on a book project entitled "The Unruly Everyday: Managing Housing, Home, and the Russian City, 1890–1935."

Abdur Razzaque Khan, Ph.D., is an associate professor in the Department of Mass Communication and Journalism at the University of Dhaka, Bangladesh. Dr Abdur Razzaque Khan earned his Ph.D. degree from the Journalism and Media Studies Centre (JMSC) at the University of Hong Kong (HKU). He completed his Ph.D. at JMSC, Hong Kong University. Earlier, Khan taught for 16 years at the University of Chittagong and was the Chair (Head) of the

Department of Communication and Journalism. He worked in journalism for 12 years before joining academia. Khan's works and interests include Critical theory, the political economy of media and communication, communication and social justice, subaltern communication and journalism, media and crony capitalism, religion and social media, and qualitative research.

Ahmed Abidur Razzaque Khan alias Ahmed Abid, Ph.D., is a filmmaker. He is currently an Assistant Professor of general education at the University of Liberal Arts Bangladesh (ULAB), as well as a member of the Humanitarian and Development Research Initiative (HADRI) at the School of Social Sciences, Western Sydney University, Australia. He completed his Ph.D. in Human Rights, Society, and Multi-level Governance at Western Sydney University. He has more than eighteen years of experience in academic and development work around Asia and the Pacific. His research disciplines focus on new and alternative media, migration, refugees, and labour trafficking.

Alex Moore is a Ph.D. student at the University of Galway, Ireland, in political science and sociology, and his thesis is on far-right sociopolitical movements. He completed two master's degrees in politics, economics, philosophy, and comparative social research at the National Research University Higher School of Economics. He has participated in study abroad programmes in North Korea, and his areas of interest include post-truth philosophy, populism, conspiracy theories, social movements, and political manifestos/ideologies.

Feeza Vasudeva is the Academy Researcher at the Faculty of Theology, University of Helsinki, Finland. Her work lies at the intersection of religion, political culture, and technology. Currently, she is exploring the role of Generative AI within religious contexts.

Monika Verma is a MSCA-CZ postdoctoral fellow at the Myanmar Studies Center, Department of Asian Studies, Palacký University Olomouc, Czech Republic. She earned her Ph.D. from the Institute of Social Research and Cultural Studies at National Yang-Ming Chiao Tung University, Taiwan. Her research has been published in several peer-reviewed journals, including the *International Journal of Population Studies*, *Innovation in the Social Sciences*, and *Asia Review* (아시아리뷰). Her work focuses on refugees and forced migration in South Asia, with her current research examining the securitization of migration in the region and its impact on Rohingya refugees.

Liudmila Nikolaevna Zhdanovich is an associate professor at the Higher School of Philosophy, History and Social Sciences, Immanuel Kant Baltic Federal University (Kaliningrad). Her education and degrees include 1999—Degree in History, Kaliningrad State University; 2005—Candidate of Sciences (Ph.D.) in National History, Yaroslav-the-Wise Novgorod State University. Her thesis is titled "Officials on Peasant Affairs in Northwest provinces of Russia in 1861–1904." Her academic interests are in the field of Agrarian history of post-reform Russia, Ethnic and National Politics of the Russian Empire in the 19th to the beginning of the 20th century, and the history of Eastern Prussia and the Kaliningrad region.

PREFACE

Social theories in the contemporary world mainly come from the Euro-American world, and here we do not get the dynamics of social thinking from other parts of the world. In this book, we explore Russian social thought in the 19th century as part of our effort to understand social theorizing in our contemporary world historically as well as from theoretical movements from different parts of the world. The book is part of our book series, Social Thought, Regional Imagination and Planetary Conversations, edited by Ananta Kumar Giri.

We are offering this work at a critical juncture in Russian and world history with the Russian invasion of Ukraine in 2022 and the subsequent war between Russia and Ukraine and the challenges of NATO expansionism and American hegemony. There is a need to understand Russia better, and our exploration hopefully helps us in this direction.

We are grateful to Aakash Singh Rathore, our friend at Routledge, for his consideration and support for this project.

Ananta Kumar Giri, Artem Uldanov, Sergey Parkhomenko,
Arnab Roy Chowdhury and Deirdre Ruscitti Harshman
June 6, 2025

AN INTRODUCTION AND
AN INVITATION

*Ananta Kumar Giri, Artem Uldanov, Sergey Parkhomenko,
Arnab Roy Chowdhury, and Deirdre Ruscitti Harshman*

There is an opinion that Russian social theory is secondary to the European one and lacks originality. According to Vvedenskiy, such opinions has sometimes led to radical statements that Russians by nature were not disposed to: "...as if they by nature were too sober and straightforward about things to venture into philosophical abstractions" (Vvedenskiy, 1898, p. 4). In particular, B. Yakovenko wrote that the lack of characteristic features of Russian social thought is related to its "lack of originality" (Yakovenko, 2008, p. 16). Of course, Russian thinkers and social theorists built their ideas on the already existing foundation of European philosophy, religion, and science. Russia was not an intellectual periphery, but it did not set trends, by and large. This was partly due to the "catching-up" nature of Russian scientific thought in general. Russian social thought in the 19th century was characterized by a certain old-fashionedness; it relied on philosophy and religion and saw in social development deeper themes related to human nature, religion, and moral choice. The schools of social theory that were practiced in the Russian Empire were created as part of a larger universe of social thought (Vucinich, 1976). Its formation, structural place, and practical involvement in social transformation have given it some distinct features: a holistic view of social phenomena and crises; moral concepts of relations between society and the state; and an emphasis on justice, crime, and punishment, along with the integral concept of personality (Medushevskiy, 2015).

One of the features of Russian social thought is related to the relationship between church and state in Russian society over the course of history. The strong influence of the state on the church was institutionalized under Peter the Great and turned the church into a kind of ministry under the

DOI: 10.4324/9781003541004-1

government. This subordinate position added certain features even to religious philosophy. Everything has its place; there must be a harmony between *ratio* and *fides*. As Mikhail Lomonosov, one of the founders of Russian science and a leading figure of the 18th century Russian Enlightenment wrote: "A mathematician is wrong if he wants to measure God's will with a compass, but neither is a theologian right if he thinks that one can learn astronomy or chemistry from the Psalter" (Lomonosov, 1952, p. 311). The idea that religion, science, and culture must coexist and nourish the development of a prosperous society had strong roots in Russian social thought of that time. Uncontrollable technical and social progress must be guided by Christian values, but at the same time this progress could lead to a better future where the environment is more fruitful to preserve these values.

Russian social theory of the 19th century is closely interlinked with the concepts of natural philosophy and idealism. Moreover, it is inconceivable without the German influence and, first of all, without the influence of Friedrich Schelling. As Gyuliga noted,

> Neither Kant nor Fichte, but Schelling was destined to become the ruler of Russian philosophical thought and to have a significant influence on the development of Russian thinkers until the end of the XIX century. Schelling meant more to Russia than to Germany.
>
> *(Gyuliga, 1984, p. 289)*

The first major disseminator of Schelling's ideas in Russia was the "Society of Lyubomudriye" (Общество любомудрия) (Kamensky, 1980). It was a secret society consisting of young men from different noble families. All of them received excellent education, and almost all of them were men of distinguished talents. When they became close friends while serving in the archive of the Ministry of Foreign Affairs in Moscow, they immediately agreed on their interest in philosophy. Just at that time, Mikhail Pavlov, a prominent disciple of Schelling and one of the professors of Moscow University, returned from abroad and enthusiastically began to familiarize his students with Schelling's philosophy. Some of these students were members of the "Society." Their interest in philosophy and receptiveness to new knowledge were very fruitful grounds for the ideas of Schelling that were taught by Pavlov and some other professors (Nosov, 1981). From 1831, the main centre of perception of Schelling's ideas (together with the ideas of other German philosophers) became the circle of N. Stankevich, in which A. Herzen, V. Belinsky, M. Bakunin, K. Aksakov took part. It is a difficult task to explain the exact reason why Schelling became so popular among Russian intellectuals at that time. Many of them tried to "transplant" his ideas to Russian soil. In Russian thought, God, as a concept of pure reason, was considered something very arguable. There was a revolt against the philosophy of religion within reason. Apollo Grigoriev said that Schelling was "life, not theory" (Grigoriev, 1980, p. 261). Many of the poems of Fyodor Tyutchev were written under Schelling's influence, and moreover, he was personally acquainted with Schelling (Toporov, 1990). Schellingianism, as a philosophical movement, gave rise to the origins of Slavophilism, which is clearly seen in the reflection of Schelling's thoughts in the works of Russian philosophers. Schelling's philosophy influenced the work and spiritual development of P. Chaadaev, F. Dostoevsky, L. Tolstoy, P. Yurkevich, and F. Tyutchev (Saharov, 1977). His philosophy of art played a role in the formation of Russian romanticism. The religious and mystical aspirations of F. Schelling are reflected in the works of V. S. Soloviev. In Russia, Schelling was loved for limiting the place of knowledge and giving place to faith and for the fact that he turned the absolute, an empty word of Western philosophy, into a person who lives his divine life, the living God (Giryonok, 1990).

The development of social thought in Russia is related not only to the peculiarities of Russian history but also to the country's geographic position. Geography had a strong influence on Russian self-determination, with its West-East dilemma, which was most vividly expressed in the confrontation between the so-called "Westerners" and "Slavophiles." The "unique Russian way" was reflected in the writings of Russian social philosophers, and the striking contradiction between the West and the East, of which Russia has been a part for almost its entire history, only reinforced the doubts of Russian thinkers. It is important to note, however, that the Asian influence in Russia should be understood to a greater extent as Byzantium influence, which can only conventionally be classified as Asian, rather than any other countries or cultures. The Byzantine Empire indirectly served as a prototype for the creation of the Russian Empire, and the religious influence of the Byzantine Church laid the foundation for Russian religious philosophy.

The problem of Russia's uncertain status as a periphery of Europe has been a major challenge for the Russian elites since the famous reforms of Peter the Great, but the initial interpretation of this problem was not very controversial. According to popular wisdom, Russia was lagging behind the West in terms of growth, but as a "young country," it has a good chance of quickly closing the gap. Attempts to mindlessly copy the Western norms and customs were ridiculed, but at the same time it was clear to Russian aristocracy that the country needs to learn from more developed societies. This hopeful and widely accepted attitude was challenged after the Napoleonic Wars, when the disputes between the representatives of the Russian state and part of the educated elites became more escalated. The latter group seeks faster modernization of society and meaningful political changes while the Czar and the state considered such ideas as dangerous and inadequate. The debate over Russia's "special way," "historical destiny," "place in European politics," "unique spirituality," and the relative benefits and drawbacks of its "backwardness" in comparison to the West was particularly heated during the first ten years of Nicholas I's reign, which was marked with such important events as the Decembrist uprising in 1825 and the November Uprising in Poland in 1830.

As Pavel Sorokin noted in regard to the context that shaped Russian social thought at this time: "...the golden age of progressive high culture coexisted with an outworn institutional system" (Sorokin, 2015, p. 344).

Following the release of Peter Chaadayev's "First Philosophical Letter" in 1836, the debate grew even more intense. Chaadayev claims that Russia's erroneous decision to make Eastern Christianity the official religion caused it to be isolated from both the Islamic East and the Catholic West, and that it was unable to integrate naturally into either of the major civilizations of the globe (Losskiy, 1991). The letter was published at the same time when Sergei Uvarov, Minister of National Education, developed the new official ideology of the Russian Empire, known as "Orthodoxy, Autocracy, and *Narodnost*" (*Nationalgeist*). According to Uvarov, Russia was spared the degradation that the contemporary West had to endure because of *Narodnost'*, which was characterized by loyalty to the tenets of the established political system and confession of the dogmas of the dominating religion. Prince Vyazemsky, a member of the literary society "Arzamas" and a friend of Uvarov, came up with the notion itself. Vyazemsky helped develop the "State Charter of the Russian Empire," which was an analogue of the Constitution that Alexander I had suggested. While working on this issue he had to deal with the problem of the Russian political language's underdevelopment and lack of definitions for several important terms. For example, the French concept of *nationalité* allowed the European monarchies of the time to understand their own power through a unique relationship to the nation and its citizens, but in Russia there was no such concept developed. Being in Poland, Vyazemsky noticed that there is a specific term called *narodowość* already existing in Polish, so he decided to utilize this term and introduce it in Russian as *Narodnost'*. The new term linked the two French words *populaire* and *national*: "folk" as referring to the life of the people, such as the peasants or inhabitants of pre-Peter Russia, and "national" as a characteristic of all social strata in general. At the same time, it has been unclear what the exact meaning of this concept is. Almost twenty years later, Belinsky noticed that the term was used universally, but its meaning remained mostly dark and mysterious. It referred to other, more significant values that have not been fully conceptualized yet (Belinsky, 1979).

When Uvarov became minister of education in 1833, he tried to solve the problem of the uncertainty and "enigma" of the term and interpreted it through the other two elements of the triad. Russian *Narodnost'* thus consisted in adherence to Orthodoxy and adherence to a monarchical mode of government. Moreover, Uvarov was convinced that Russia and Europe are moving in the same direction, which is set by European values, in particular science and education. However, Russia is moving towards "European civilization" in a special way that is different from the trajectories of the revolution-weakened "old" Europe. The Tsar's power was nationally acclaimed because it was the result of a centuries-long process of historical development, from the calling of the Varangians and the baptism of Rus' to the war of 1812. Russian *Narodnost'* is thus rooted in history. These conflicting doctrines were amplified by the ongoing debate between the so-called "Westernism" and "Slavophilism" movements in Russian socio-political thought. During the heated salon discussions about the meaning of Chaadayev's publication both parties formulated their own vision of Russia's future. From the perspective of "Westerners," Russia can only expect to effectively compete with its European neighbours in terms of politics, economy, and culture after finishing the process of Westernization. Slavophiles, on the other hand, held that Russia had a "special way" that was rooted in its pre-Petrine heritage,[1] Orthodox spirituality, and communal spirit. Official ideology supporters had access to all available resources and used censorship and overt police repression to limit the expression of opposing viewpoints. Their opponents promoted their beliefs through literature and self-published articles, and they arranged their debates in closed salons and clubs. Literature and its critical interpretations played a pivotal part in these debates since it was replete with references and clues about the prevailing socio-political controversy. The public discussion around Gogol's Dead Souls regarding Russia's mission and historical destiny is among the most striking instances of this type of argument. Adherents of both doctrines hastened to enlist the writer as one of their supporters. "Westerners," led by the famous literature critic Belinsky, insisted that Gogol's work is a ferocious denunciation of Russian society; Slavophile critics saw this publication as a rampant apotheosis of Russian culture and society.

Both "Westerners" and "Slavophiles" seek to develop universal arguments in support of their position, and to do so they tried to assess different positive and negative features of the European influence over Russia. Some Russian thinkers like Odoevskiy or Kireevskiy saw a downside in European philosophy in its "one-sidedness." According to Odoevsky,

But God save us to concentrate all our mental, moral, and physical powers on one material direction, however useful it may be: whether it be railroads, paper spinning mills, cloth mills or chintz factories. One-sidedness is the poison of today's societies and the secret cause of all complaints, unrest and perplexities; when one branch lives on the expense of the whole tree, the tree withers away.

(Odoevskiy, 1913, p. 65)

This universal one-sidedness, as Odoevskiy believed, is a consequence of rationalistic schematism, which is unable to offer any complete and holistic understanding of nature, history, and person. According to Odoevskiy, only symbolic cognition can bring us closer to comprehending. In addition, this demand for a more holistic approach is reflected in Russian social thought and literature. There are three elements that are fused in a person—believing, cognitive, and aesthetic. These elements can and should form a harmonious unity not only in the human soul but also in public life. It is this kind of wholeness that Odoevskiy and many other Russian philosophers did not find in the 19th century's civilization (Losskiy, 1991).

It would be incorrect to reduce these debates to purely theoretical mind games and a sort of hobby for wealthy and well-educated people. Both "Westerners" and "Slavophiles" desired to implement their ideas in practice to fight against injustices and the "backwardness" of their homeland. In the 1840s, both intellectual movements made attempts to form a plan to abolish serfdom in Russia and to formulate their vision for further reforms. But for the "Slavophiles" the development of Russia was not an issue of some standards that were established in Western Europe and must be simply met in the Russian Empire, but rather a step on the way to true "Sobornost'." In their opinion, this concept is the most essential characteristic of Russian society that is closely connected with Eastern Christianity's religious legacy. According to the "Slavophiles," only Orthodoxy has embraced and preserved the eternal truth of early Christianity in its entirety, namely the idea of the identity of unity and freedom. This is reflected in the idea of "Sobornost'"—the free unity of believers in their joint understanding of the truths of Orthodoxy and in the joint search for the way to salvation. This is the way to organize a just and moral society that is not affected by the "one-sidedness" of Western civilization and not stretched by the "old-fashionedness" of Eastern influence. This endless search for an understanding of the role and place of Russia between West and East could be traced in the works of very different Russian social thinkers and in the great Russian literature of the 19th century (Zhereb, 2017). It is not a coincidence that one of the brightest figures among the Russian "Westerners" was Vissarion Belinsky—a famous literary critic.

Art, philosophy, and religion were closely intertwined, and this is why philosophical ideas were reflected in Russian literature in such a significant way. Hence, the fact that, for foreigners, the most famous social thinkers of the time were the Russian writers, Tolstoy and Dostoevsky, rather than the philosophers Bakunin or Stronin, for example. This may seem strange, since Russian writers were not detached from social and political discussions and drew on the ideas of Russian social and religious philosophers in their texts. Why, then, did Russian literature gain worldwide recognition while Russian social thought did not? In itself, this question is already incorrect because it artificially separates Russian philosophy and literature, which are closely linked in the Russian tradition.

This volume seeks to provide the readers with information about these concepts and ideas, which are specific to Russian socio-philosophic thought, and also present the key figures of Russian social theory in the 19th century, those whose ideas directly or indirectly inspired famous Russian authors of the 19th and even the 20th centuries, and those who looked for answers to both philosophical and practical issues of human society's development. The Russian variant of social theory, which is the topic of this volume, dwells heavily on the concept of social reality. As a result of this emphasis, although the Russian social thinkers of the second half of the 19th and of the early 20th centuries are generally considered sociologists, their ideas and conceptualizations link into a much broader and interdisciplinary conversation. The type of general social theory discussed in our book includes philosophical provisions, varied theories of social structures and processes, alongside concerns relevant to contemporary sociologists (Reznik, 2007).

Note

1 Peter the Great introduced significant reforms in Russia at the beginning of the 18th century. They were aimed at the modernization of the country and the development of its economy, social order, and military capacity. He studied from European experience and replaced traditional Russian customs with European ones. Also, he invited foreigners to modernize the administration practices and the military standards and to push forward Russian science. These radical changes affected the development of Russia for a long time and were considered quite controversial because, together with the positive effects, they also eradicated some traditional Russian social institutes.

References

Belinsky, V. *Selected Works*, Moscow: Soviet Literature, 1979. 384 p. [In Russian]
Giryonok, F. Russkiy Cosmism. Moscow: Znanie, 1990. 182 p. [In Russian]
Grigoriev, A. Aesthetic and Critic. Moscow: Iskusstvo, 1980. 496 p. [In Russian]
Gyuliga, A. Schelling. Moscow. Molodaya Gvardiya, 1984. 317 p. [In Russian]
Kamensky, Z. Moskovskiy kruzhok lubomudrov. Moscow: Nauka. 1980. 327 p. [In Russian]
Lomonosov, M. Complete Works: Volume 7: Works on Philology, Moscow: Izdatel'stvo AN USSR, 1952. 1000 p. [In Russian]
Losskiy, N. History of Russian Philosophy. Moscow: Sovetskiy Pisatel', 1991. 482 p. [In Russian]

Medushevskiy, A. History of Russian sociology, Direct-Media, 2015. 497 p. [In Russian]

Nosov, A. Philosophy and Aesthetics of the 'Lyubomudry.' *Voprosy literatury*, no. 9 (1981): 247–256. [In Russian]

Odoevskiy, V. *Russkiye nochi [Russian Nights]*. Moscow: Put' Publishing, 1913, 437 p. [In Russian]

Reznik, Y. Russia Needs More Philosophy. *Lichnost' Kultura Obschestvo* 9, no. 2 (36) (2007): 122–130. [In Russian]

Saharov, V. Bytovanie Schellingianskih Idey v Russkoy Literature. *Context*, 1977: 210–226. [In Russian]

Sorokin, P. The Russian Sociological Tradition from the XIXth Century Until the Present: Key Features and Possible Value for Current Discussions. *The American Sociologist* 46 (2015): 341–355.

Toporov, V. Zametki o poezii Tutcheva. Tallin: Tutchevskiy Sbornik, 1990. 161 p. [In Russian]

Vucinich, A. Social Thought in Tsarist Russia: The Quest for a General Science of Society, 1861–1917. Chicago and London: University of Chicago Press, 1976. 294 p.

Vvedenskiy, A. Sud'by filosofii v Rossii, Moscow: Kushnerev & Co, 1898. 43 p. [In Russian]

Yakovenko, I. Undertsanding Russia: Civilizational Analysis, Moscow: Nauka, 2008. 521 p. [In Russian]

Zhereb, A. The Development of Russian Sociology in the Period Between the Second Half of the 19th Century and the Beginning of the 20th Century. European Scientific Journal, 13, no. 10. (2017).

1

FROM SOCIOLOGICAL TO GEOGRAPHICAL THOUGHTS OF LEV ILYICH MECHNIKOV

Society and the law of cooperation

Monika Verma

Lev Ilyich Mechnikov (1838–1888)

Lev IlyichMechnikov, the son of Ilya Ivanovich Mechnikov and elder brother of the renowned Russian biologist and Nobel laureate Ilya Mechnikov, was born in Saint Petersburg, Russia, on May 30, 1838 (White, 1976). He completed his primary and secondary education in Petersburg and enrolled at the Petersburg School of Law in 1850. However, he developed hip joint inflammation, known as coxitis, which forced him to leave the university in 1852. Following this setback, he moved to Panasovka (Ukraine) to continue his studies. In August 1856, he entered Kharkiv University to study medicine, but his involvement in student disturbances led to his expulsion. He then continued his medical studies at the Medico-Surgical Academy and later at St. Petersburg University (White, 1976). Mechnikov's interests extended beyond law and medicine to foreign languages, prompting him to enrol at the Institute of Oriental Languages, where he mastered "10 European and 3 Eastern (Arabic, Persian, and Turkish) languages" (Andreev, 2019: 8). His repeated involvement in student disturbances led to his expulsion from St. Petersburg University as well.

Due to his financial insecurities and repeated expulsions from universities, Lev Mechnikov moved to the Middle East, where he worked as a translator on "a Russian diplomatic mission to the Near East" (White, 1976: 396). He also served as a sales agent for a Russian trade company. In March 1860, he relocated to Venice, Italy, to study the arts and painting. During this period, he met the revolutionary army General J. Garibaldi and joined Garibaldi's army as a lieutenant, participating in the liberation of Naples. He fought in the Battle of Volturno, where he was severely wounded by an

DOI: 10.4324/9781003541004-2

exploding mine. Mechnikov also took part in the efforts to liberate Slavic peoples from Austrian and Turkish rule (White, 1976).

During these liberation wars, he became acquainted with Russian revolutionary anarchist Mikhail Alexandrovich Bakunin and conducted propaganda campaigns for anarchists in Italy and Spain. His involvement in the liberation wars and anarchist propaganda led him to pursue a career in journalism in 1861. This marked a turning point in Mechnikov's career, as he began publishing numerous articles, reviews, and opinions on social and political issues from an anarchist perspective. At the same time, he became a member of "the center of the Russian emigration" and participated in "the anarchist section of the First International" in 1864 (Andreev, 2019: 8).

In April 1874, Lev Mechnikov moved to Japan at the invitation of the Japanese Minister of Education to teach Russian to Japanese students. He led the Russian language branch of the Tokyo School of Foreign Languages for over a year and a half. Upon his return, he compiled his experiences in Japan into a manuscript titled *"L'Empire Japonais,"* illustrated with his own drawings and sketches (Mechnikov, 1881, cited in White, 1976).

At the end of 1875, Mechnikov returned to Switzerland, where he became a professor of statistics and comparative geography at the Academy of Neuchâtel. He published numerous articles on topics such as economics, sociology, psychology, critical reviews, political analyses, and essays on the history of civilization (Andreev, 2019). He passed away in Clarens, Switzerland, in June 1888 (Andreev, 2019). The final years of his lectures at Neuchâtel were compiled by his friend and colleague Élisée Reclus, a French geographer and anarchist, into a book titled *"La Civilisation et les grands fleuves historiques"* (Civilization and the Great Historical Rivers), published posthumously in France in 1889. The book presents a "theory of human development and lays the foundations of geopolitics as a science" (Andreev, 2019: 10).

Lev Mechnikov: revolutionary anarchist

An explicit explanation of Mechnikov's understanding of "society" and the analysis of complex social phenomena can be found in his significant sociological works such as "Revolution and Evolution" (1886) and "Civilization and the Great Historical Rivers[1]" (2013). Highly sceptical of power and authority, Mechnikov rejected all involuntary and coercive forms of hierarchy. He argued, "a great deal of evil, ignorance, brute force and arbitrariness inhere in all of our social institutions" (White, 1976: 397).

As an anarchist, Mechnikov's political thoughts aligned with prominent anarchists of his time, including Élisée Reclus, Mikhail Bakunin, and Peter Kropotkin. His voyages and lifelong struggles brought him close to these figures, shaping and inspiring his social and political views. Bakunin's ideas strongly influenced Mechnikov's anarchism, and there were many similarities in their writings. For instance, Bakunin repudiated authority and coercion in every form, believing they led to enslavement. He argued that "all tormentors, oppressors, and exploiters of humanity, such as priests, monarchs, statesmen, soldiers, financiers, officials, policemen, gendarmes, jailers, executioners, monopolists, and politicians, contributed to this enslavement" (Bakunin, 1970: 17). Bakunin saw the church and the state as the primary institutions of human's enslavement, calling them "my two bêtes noires" (Bakunin, 1970: 34). He contended that every state has been an instrument by which a privileged few wielded power over the vast majority, and every church has been a loyal ally of the state in subjugating mankind. Governments throughout history have used religion to keep humanity in ignorance and as a "safety-valve" for their misery and frustration (Bakunin, 1970: vii).

Mechnikov believed that the "absence of authority does not imply that society will break down into lawless anarchy where the weak are at the mercy of the strong" (White, 1976: 401). Instead, the removal of authority would allow the "law of cooperation" to come into full play (White, 1976: 401). He argued that society is not a stable entity but one that is constantly shaped and reshaped. The cooperative culture of "mutual aid" or "cooperative behaviour" during the Meiji Ishin (the Meiji Restoration) in Japan enabled him to envision a global application of cooperative civilizational development.

Scholar James D. White was curious about the role of the state in Mechnikov's theory if the essence of society is free association. He questioned whether the state is a sociological or non-sociological entity. Mechnikov believed that "society itself undergoes a peculiar evolution in which elements of compulsion are gradually discarded until the goal of complete voluntary association is reached" (White, 1976: 401). He argued further that "more primitive societies will, therefore, be distinguished by the presence of a greater degree of compulsion, and more advanced societies with less, so social evolution would naturally culminate in the complete anarchy of free cooperation" (White, 1976: 401).

Revolution meets Ishin: Lev Mechnikov in Japan

As an anarchist and revolutionary, Mechnikov received an invitation to Japan to observe the Meiji Ishin, or Meiji Revolution, or Meiji Restoration. His journey to Japan marked a pivotal moment in his career, as it was upon his return that he formulated the law of cooperation as a fundamental factor in the development of human society, proposing it as a universal principle.

During Meiji Ishin, many European and American intellectuals and observers believed that Western nation-states played a crucial role in initiating modernization in Japan (Konishi, 2013: 31). However, for Mechnikov, Meiji Ishin represented a complete and radical revolution (Konishi, 2013: 29). He viewed it not only as a product of social and cultural advancements but also as a dynamic model of civilizational progress (Konishi, 2013: 30–2).

Mechnikov was particularly impressed by the cooperative self-organization practices among commoners during the Ishin. These cooperative efforts provided "economic and social stability to commoners' lives at a time of tremendous political instability, lack of organization guidance from above, and sudden displacement to urban areas" (Konishi, 2013: 30). Reflecting on his experience, Mechnikov argued that the Ishin was not merely a reactionary political response, but a complex revolution rooted in centuries of social, cultural, and intellectual developments, catalyzed by external disruptions (Konishi, 2013: 29). In Japan, Mechnikov saw mutual aid and voluntary cooperative associations as progressive tendencies, evidence that social revolution emerged from cumulative social and intellectual evolution (Konishi, 2013: 51).

Sho Konishi's analysis suggests that Mechnikov's time in Japan fostered a dialectical relationship between the concepts of *"Ishin"* and *"revoluitsiia,"* leading to a new understanding of Ishin as an expression of cooperative civilization that profoundly influenced his vision of human society. Mechnikov's original notion of *"revoliutsiia"* merged with the realities of Ishin, reshaping anarchist thought from a Bakuninist ideology advocating violent destruction of existing social and political structures to an evolutionary framework of civilizational development based on mutual aid (Konishi, 2013: 30). In other words, it shifted from advocating ruthless destruction to envisioning universal human evolutionary progress (Konishi, 2013: 60).

For Mechnikov, revolution was not merely dependent on a nation's material development or the maturity of its proletariat, as per Marx's philosophy, but rather on social and cultural achievements. The Japanese revolution exemplified this by evolving from the everyday lives of its people, enabling the establishment of a new government (Konishi, 2013: 61). Rather than merely emulating Westernization, Japan's rapid modernization during Ishin became a model rooted in cooperative values for Mechnikov. He viewed the foundation of human progress as cooperative human relations and spontaneous associations among people, contrasting with reliance on law and state governance, which he saw as marking the beginning of a new human history (Konishi, 2013: 59).

The law of cooperation: Mechnikov's sociological ideas

Through his sociological analysis, Mechnikov posed some fundamental questions: What defines society? What embodies the essence of sociological phenomena? What are the interrelations between the biological and sociological realms? He viewed societies as "continuously evolving expressions of the laws of nature" (Konishi, 2013: 65).

Mechnikov's theory of evolution encompassed three spheres governing the world: the inorganic, biological, and sociological. The inorganic sphere, influenced by Newtonian gravity, explains physical and chemical processes where individual elements appear unified by a universal principle of gravitation. The biological sphere involves the organic realm of plant and animal species, whose complexity and variability transcend simple gravitational laws, as articulated by Darwin in his seminal work, *On the Origin of Species* (1958). Darwinism profoundly influenced modern scientific and philosophical thought, shaping diverse disciplines. The sociological sphere, according to Mechnikov, operates under the "law of cooperation," encompassing associations, networks, interests, and collectives that include both humans and non-humans (Mechnikov, 1886: 432–433). This sphere extends beyond individual biological existence, illustrating how these spheres intricately overlap and interconnect in his worldview.

The law of evolution illustrates a fundamental principle of unity and continuity, yet there exists no clear boundary where natural science transitions into biology, and where biology transitions into sociology. Biology examines the realm of flora and fauna, focusing on phenomena like the struggle for existence, while sociology is concerned with manifestations of solidarity and the unification of forces (cooperation in nature). At the cellular level, organic matter demonstrates the ability to sustain itself by absorbing suitable elements from the environment, grow through nutrition, and ultimately divide into parts identical to the original organism. These cells also remain attached to the mother cell, thus forming a "collective organism," marking the inception of the evolution of organic forms (Mechnikov, 2013: 86). The imperative of nourishment, pervasive throughout the organic world, drives the struggle for existence, which prompts organisms to adapt to diverse environmental conditions (Mechnikov, 2013). However, Darwin's theory does not fully elucidate what role the struggle for existence plays in a phenomenon that should be considered as the point of departure for the evolution of organic forms. Darwin argued that biological evolution is governed by the struggle for existence and natural selection, asserting that humans living in societies and creating culture are fundamentally biological beings subject to the selection of kin (Mechnikov, 2013: 88).

While Darwin and his followers view the struggle for existence as the fundamental law of both biology and social life, Mechnikov emphasizes that the hallmark of social life is "the law of cooperation." In sociology, individuals unite their efforts to achieve common objectives. Cooperation, the pooling of efforts, is seen by Mechnikov as a necessary and logical outcome of the struggle for life. While cooperation may initially arise from selfish interests, its principle fundamentally differs from and opposes Darwinian struggle. The principle of cooperation diverges from the principle of struggle (Mechnikov, 2013: 142).

Drawing from the sociological sphere, Mechnikov defines society as increasingly intricate and expanding networks of cooperative associations (Konishi, 2013: 65). Sociologists across different epochs and perspectives have focused extensively on the relationship between individuals and society during various stages of social evolution. According to Mechnikov, sociological evolution progresses through three stages: first, mechanical constraint; second, subordination; and third, consensus marked by conscious and voluntary cooperation. The initial stage represents the lowest level of individualized (biological) existence, characterized by what he terms as "despotism," which then leads to subsequent stages of subordination. To achieve the voluntary stage, akin to what he terms anarchy—a state where autonomous individuals cooperate freely without external constraints—one must pass through subordination either by the specialization of labour or political tyranny on one hand. On the other hand, Mechnikov emphasizes that such cooperation is not enforced by mechanical or physiological means, nor by political authority, but rather arises solely from personal conscience and free will, as understood in modern psychology (Mechnikov, 1886: 435).

Mechnikov contends that "the law of the future society is anarchy, and that it surely shall be attained by nature left alone" (Mechnikov, 1886: 436). He argues:

> Nature requires solidarity in beings, without which she would be unable to bring about the higher forms of the future, she, first of all, habituates them to the communal life of coercion, she then softens them by differentiation, and finally, when she has judged them ripe for voluntary collaboration in their work, she lets go the reins of constraints and subordination and leaves reproduction, the most important task from a biological point of view to their most private and arbitrary instincts and inclinations.
>
> *(White, 1976: 403)*

The classical sociological theory of "society" heavily draws upon the concept of "evolution," rooted in Darwinian evolutionary theory, which was endorsed by proponents such as Auguste Comte and Herbert Spencer. Darwin's theory of natural selection, considered the fundamental law of biological evolution, posited that an animal's traits determined its likelihood of survival and reproduction, thereby influencing the prevalence of those traits in subsequent generations (Turner & McCaffree, 2021: 83). Spencer expanded on this with the concept of "survival of the fittest," asserting it as the primary law of progress in human society (Spencer, 2019: 185).

Contrary to the social Darwinist view of relentless competition, Mechnikov critiques the "survival of the fittest," which he believes leads to the eventual extinction of weaker social elements (Konishi, 2013: 65). Instead, he proposes the "law of cooperation" as a significant factor in the evolution of human societies, offering an alternative perspective in social science evolution theories. Mechnikov argues that cooperation, whether among individual cells or human beings, drives societal evolution through unity and continuity, distinct from Darwin's natural selection and the struggle for existence. He underscores that while the struggle for life may prompt individuals or animals to form societies, this interaction illustrates the intersection of biology and sociology (White, 1976: 400).

Mechnikov's sociological theory is often seen as a pivotal link between the theories of Auguste Comte and Herbert Spencer. Comte's approach to sociology begins with human beings, asserting that "social science applies only to human beings" (White, 1976: 398). Mechnikov challenges Comte's assertion by arguing that social phenomena are not exclusive to humans but are observable in the lives of animals and plants as well. He criticizes Comte's arbitrary selection of the human individual as the starting point of sociological inquiry.

Comte distinguishes between the biological and sociological realms through egoistic and altruistic instincts. He places egoistic instincts within the domain where activities are driven by the need for nutrition or personal preservation, while altruistic instincts, inherent in all living beings, mark the beginning of sociology where biological egoism gives way to altruism (Mechnikov, 2013: 102). And the physiological roots of altruism lie in sexual attraction—the association of male and female. According to Mechnikov, Comte's significant contribution to social science lies in emphasizing the aggregation of individuals through association or cooperation (conscious or unconscious). Association or cooperation, the unification of more or less numerous efforts of individuals to achieve a common goal, is already found among the primary multicellular organisms, almost at the very beginning of organic life (Mechnikov, 2013: 146).

Mechnikov extends Comte's sociological framework, arguing that sociology encompasses not only human phenomena but any form of association. He posits that wherever there is association, there is ground for sociological study, even at the most rudimentary levels of evolution, where organisms themselves can be considered as societies (White, 1976: 398). He emphasized that while all bodies share a common organismic nature, it's crucial not to overlook that organisms in plants and animals are significantly more complex than minerals. Charles Darwin and Karl von Baer explained biological phenomena through the laws of struggle for existence and differentiation. However, societies represent far greater complexity than plants and animals.

Therefore, it's reasonable and necessary to acknowledge that the challenges of sociology cannot be fully addressed by biological laws alone. In other words, "while biological laws explain biological phenomena, societies are far more complex entities that require sociological laws for comprehension" (Mechnikov, 2013: 142).

Herbert Spencer builds upon Comte's and Mechnikov's ideas, expanding the definition of sociology as a field that deals with complex social phenomena. Spencer views society as akin to a living organism, stressing the continuity between biological and sociological realms (Mechnikov, 1886: 420). He asserts that sociology represents a scientific discipline independent of biology, highlighting the intricate nature of social organization and development.

Mechnikov asserts that sociology stands as an independent science that intersects with biology. He rejects the notion that sociology is solely the study of human phenomena, arguing that social groupings based on cooperation are prevalent among animals as well. He maintains that natural science reveals association as a fundamental law of existence, with society being a specific manifestation of this broader principle (White, 1976: 398). Mechnikov contends that environmental factors stimulate the cooperative tendencies in human and animal behaviour. He emphasizes that associations for food or self-defence predominantly exhibit social cooperation rather than competition. Mechnikov argues that survival of the fittest is achieved not through individual or collective competition, but through social solidarity in overcoming challenges. He posits that in confronting the harsh conditions of the physical and geographical environment, humanity faces a stark choice: solidarity or demise. He asserts that collective labour and solidarity are essential for human civilization's successful development, representing the foundational law of progress (Mechnikov, 2013: 276).

Mechnikov's theory of the "law of cooperation" resonates closely with the ideas of Russian anarchist Peter Kropotkin. While Darwin's theory emphasizes the struggle for life as a key driver of evolution, Kropotkin proposes "the law of mutual aid" as central to evolutionary success. According to Kropotkin, the progressive evolution of species relies more on mutual cooperation than on competitive struggle (Kropotkin, 1989: xxxviii). He critiques the notion that intense competition alone drives evolutionary progress, arguing instead for the importance of cooperative behaviours in fostering species advancement (Kropotkin, 1989: xxxvii). Similarly, Mechnikov's concept of the law of cooperation aligns with Kropotkin's theory of mutual aid, both challenging Darwin's emphasis on competition in evolutionary theory. They assert that sociology encompasses any phenomenon where cooperation plays a role, highlighting cooperation as a fundamental aspect of social and biological evolution.

According to Mechnikov, there are three fundamental principles of association or cooperation (Mechnikov, 2013: 146–147):

1. At the most basic level, among primary multicellular organisms, cooperation is characterized by simple mechanical connections that link individual cells within the organism in various ways.
2. Moving up the biological ladder, cooperation arises out of physiological necessity, driven by the fact that each individual or member cannot exist independently but requires communication and cooperation with others.
3. Finally, at the highest stage of development, cooperation takes on a more voluntary and free character. The rudimentary forms of this highest association, such as familial units (marriage groups), begin to form under influences like sexual desire, which are neither purely mechanical nor purely physiological.

This progression of social bonds starts with purely mechanical and compulsory forms and gradually evolves towards more psychological and eventually voluntary unions. Mechnikov not only demonstrates the importance of the law of cooperation in envisioning future societies through anarchism but also seeks to explain how past societies evolved using the same principle. He categorizes the historical development of peoples into three main periods (Mechnikov, 2013: 160):

1. **The period of forced associations or coercive social organizations:** Beginning with ancient despotism, this era is characterized by societies based on coercion, slavery, and the subordination of all to a single authority figure.
2. **The period of subordinate groupings and unions:** During this phase, characterized by oligarchy and feudal federations, societies witness varying degrees of social differentiation and intense class struggle, often manifesting as economic competition. This period also sees the rise of serfdom and forced labor.
3. **The period of free associations:** This era, which Mechnikov sees as emerging in the present and belonging to the future, already embodies principles such as freedom (the abolition of all coercion), equality (the elimination of unjust social and political divisions and privileges), and brotherhood (solidarity replacing conflict and disunity).

Mechnikov's perspective on human history revolves around these forms of social organization. Nature initially compelled individual organisms into collectives through coercion and necessity, then gradually acclimatized them to social life through differentiation. Ultimately, when individuals mature sufficiently for conscious and voluntary cooperation and the association of their labour, nature abolishes all forms of coercion and subordination (Mechnikov, 2013: 147). For Mechnikov, true civilization is measured by the extent of freedom pervading society. Social progress, in his view, inversely correlates with the degree of coercion, violence, or power evident in social life, and directly relates to the development of freedom and self-consciousness, which he equates with anarchy as discussed previously.

Geographical roots of ancient civilizations

Mechnikov was deeply interested in the geographical synthesis of history. He believed that the environment influences not only individuals but also entire societies. Mechnikov argued that in hot zones, no stable civilization has ever achieved lasting prominence in the annals of humankind. In the warm and humid climates of these hot zones, plants like breadfruit, date palm, and coconut palm grow abundantly, providing daily sustenance, utensils, fabrics, and fibres. While humans can thrive in these conditions, they cannot advance to higher levels of civilization because the essential condition for historical life and progress—the need for constant and strenuous work—is absent.

According to Mechnikov, the great historical civilizations are concentrated exclusively in the temperate zone. The most ancient civilizations of this temperate zone, such as the Egyptian, Assyrian-Babylonian, and the ancient Aryan cultures of Iran and India, particularly developed and flourished in subtropical regions where the average annual temperature did not fall below 22 degrees.

Most scientists of Mechnikov's time divided the earth's inhabitants into two groups (Mechnikov, 2013: 173):

Chosen Races—Groups with historical or cultural significance.
Outcast Races—Groups considered wild, savage, or barbaric.

To explain the differences in the roles these groups played in the development of culture or civilization, Mechnikov noted that modern science had created two theories. The first, the ethnological theory, attributes the uneven distribution of civilization to inherent differences in abilities among various races. The second, the geographical theory, attributes these differences to the influence of the environment. The ethnological theory is grounded in the conservative principle of heredity, while the geographical theory emphasizes evolution and adaptation to the environment.

Many natural scientists have long championed evolutionary theory, among them notable figures such as German scientists Carl Vogt, Clémence Royer, and Dr. Charles Letourneau, who ardently defended the theory of heredity. According to Letourneau, human races exhibit a hierarchical structure influenced significantly by hereditary physical and mental traits rather than environmental factors, shaping their social development (Letourneau, cited in Mechnikov, 2013: 173). He further asserted that anatomically inferior races have historically failed to create civilizations of higher order, suggesting a persistent organic disadvantage that can only be partially overcome through strenuous effort. He argued that human races vary widely in what he termed "organic nobility," with some clearly deserving the designation of "chosen," while others, by contrast, are relegated to a class of societal "outcasts" (Letourneau, cited in Mechnikov, 2013: 174).

Henry Thomas Buckle, an English historian and philosopher, proposed that early civilizations worthy of recognition flourished in regions where abundant plant resources ensured easy sustenance for human populations (Buckle, cited in Mechnikov, 2013: 174). Letourneau, while acknowledging the partial truth in Buckle's assertion, maintained that environmental conditions alone do not dictate the entire course of human destiny (Letourneau, cited in Mechnikov, 2013: 174). Letourneau categorically classified the human race into three distinct groups: the black race, viewed as hereditarily incapable of intermingling with superior races; the yellow race, represented by Mongolians and considered vastly superior to the black race; and the white race, distinguished by well-developed brain hemispheres, a straightened forehead, and reduced jaw bones, qualities the white race deemed essential for cultural and civilizational advancement. According to Letourneau's framework, only individuals of the white race possess the capacity for higher cultural achievements (Letourneau, cited in Mechnikov, 2013: 174).

Mechnikov countered Letourneau's assertion regarding the correlation between superior races and civilization. He expressed skepticism about such divisions, pointing out that despite millennia of contact with advanced civilizations, Bedouins have persisted in a state similar to that observed during the time of the pharaohs. Mechnikov highlighted that even purer Bedouin Semites, classified as representatives of a lower race by Letourneau, were responsible for creating the illustrious Assyrian-Babylonian and later Arab civilizations (Mechnikov, 2013: 177).

Mechnikov argued that the crux of the matter does not lie in racial abilities but rather in environmental conditions (Mechnikov, 2013: 178). He contended that the inability to foster higher cultures, which Letourneau attributed predominantly to the "outcast" Negro race, could also be observed in significant parts of the white race and nearly all representatives of the yellow race. In Mechnikov's view, the great historical civilizations emerged from complex amalgamations of ethnological elements where the contributions of "white," "yellow," and "black" races cannot be distinctly delineated. Rejecting Letourneau's notion that innate abilities of higher racial types facilitated progress and civilization, Mechnikov emphasized that civilizations like that of the Egyptians emerged not due to racial superiority but as a result of specific environmental and socio-economic conditions. For Mechnikov, it was these conditions, rather than racial characteristics, that fostered the development of civilization across different peoples (Mechnikov, 2013: 177–178).

Among proponents of evolutionary theory, many uphold the original hierarchy of races, contending that only the "chosen race" possesses the capacity for progress and civilization, while all others are fated to remain in perpetual barbarism and savagery (Mechnikov, 2013: 129). Mechnikov emphasized the significant role of heredity in evolution, asserting that it reinforces and transmits acquired abilities and habits across generations, influenced by environmental factors, thereby contributing to the evolution of human races. However, he argued that heredity alone cannot negate the profound impact of the environment, which exerts a more dominant influence on human development (Mechnikov, 2013: 184).

Human history, according to Mechnikov, unfolds as a continuous series of examples demonstrating how environmental conditions and the geographical features of our planet have either promoted or hindered human progress. He illustrated this with examples such as the oceans, once viewed with dread and serving to separate peoples, now functioning as conduits of international unity through trade and cultural exchange (Mechnikov, 2013: 131). For instance, the Mississippi River, integral to the economic life of the United States today, held no significance for the indigenous peoples who lived by hunting, underscoring how environmental context shapes human interactions and development (Mechnikov, 2013: 132).

In his book "*Tsivilizatsiya i velikie istoricheskie reki (Civilization and the Great Historical Rivers)*," Mechnikov intricately explores the historical epochs rooted in the basins of significant rivers. He elaborates on the concept of Oriental despotism and hydraulic societies, proposing that civilizations such as those along the Nile (Egypt), the Tigris and Euphrates (Mesopotamia), the Indus (Sindh) Valley, and the rivers of eastern China (the Yellow River and the Yangtze) were nurtured by annual floods, which served as educators to their coastal inhabitants (Mechnikov, 2013: 132).

Mechnikov argues that the nature of civilization and societal structure primarily hinges on how a people adapt to their environmental conditions (Mechnikov, 2013: 131). According to him, historical development unfolds through three distinct phases of civilization:

1. The river age: The genesis of civilization along the banks of great rivers.
2. The maritime era: When centres of civilization shifted to the shores of internal seas.
3. The oceanic era: Symbolizing the shift of global civilization centres to the Atlantic Ocean shores following the discovery of America.

He identifies the four oldest great cultures as originating from the banks of major rivers: Egyptian and Assyrian-Babylonian in the West, and Indian and Chinese in the East (Mechnikov, 2013: 199). Chinese civilization, for instance, flourished in the regions rinsed by the Yellow River and the Yangtze, while Vedic culture was confined to the basins of the Indus and Ganges. Assyrian-Babylonian civilization emerged along the Tigris and Euphrates, crucial arteries of the Mesopotamian valley, and Ancient Egypt, as noted by Herodotus, owed its existence and prosperity to the Nile (Mechnikov, 2013: 207). Mechnikov contends that rivers play a pivotal role in the birth and development of civilizations, embodying a synthesis of physical and geographical factors such as climate, soil, terrain, and geological structure. He illustrates how nature creates the Nile and its fertile qualities and how the Nile's unique characteristics contributed to Egypt's fertility and subsequent historical trajectory (Mechnikov, 2013: 229). From Egypt's earliest history, Mechnikov argues, the Nile Valley's environmental conditions fostered solidarity, collective labour, and cooperative efforts among its inhabitants, laying the foundation for Egypt's prosperity and cultural advancement. While acknowledging the profound influence of rivers in shaping human societies, Mechnikov also recognizes that a sense of solidarity can be instilled in individuals by geographical environments beyond river basins (Mechnikov, 2013: 276). Nonetheless, he posits that the example of the four great ancient civilizations serves as compelling evidence that development occurred primarily within the nurturing environment of rivers, which inspire solidarity among their inhabitants. Civilizations that originated along the banks of historic rivers were initially primitive, isolated, and distinct from one another. However, as these civilizations expanded from riverbanks to coastal regions, they gained the capacity for diffusion, further development, and gradually acquired an international character (Mechnikov, 2013: 202). The ability of civilizations to propagate and spread, already well-developed during the early Mediterranean era, increased as they transitioned from inland sea coasts to oceanic coasts. Mechnikov argued against attributing climate as the decisive factor influencing the fate of civilizations, countering the prevailing notion that societal progress hinges solely on favourable natural conditions. He posited that overly favourable environments do not necessarily spur societal advancement; rather, he demonstrated that challenges posed by adverse natural factors, such as recurring floods, compel people to unite and innovate methods of interacting with their geographic surroundings. Mechnikov assigned profound importance to rivers in the earliest stages of human society, labeling them as "the cradle of civilization." He identified a new and final phase in world history—the era of oceanic civilization—which he considered youthful compared to the preceding river and Mediterranean periods. During the Mediterranean period, characterized by hydraulic societies, the principal centres of civilization were the Mediterranean oligar-chies of Carthage, Greece, and Rome. The transition to the Middle Ages and modern times marked a swift decline in Mediterranean nations and states, juxtaposed with rapid growth in countries situated along the Atlantic Ocean coasts. This shift relocated the epicentres of civilization from Mediterranean shores to Atlantic Ocean shores. For example, Constantinople, Venice, and Genoa waned in significance while Lisbon, Paris, London, and Amsterdam emerged as leaders in cultural and intellectual movements. During this period, geographical divisions such as the Atlantic, Pacific, and Indian Oceans mark significant phases in world history. Firstly, the Atlantic Ocean played a pivotal role from the emergence of new nations up to the latter half of the 19th century. Secondly, the Pacific Ocean witnessed distinctive devel-opments, including the rapid economic growth of California and Australia, the opening of Chinese and Japanese ports for global trade, the substantial expansion of Chinese emigration, and the spread of Russian influence into Manchuria and Korea, thereby integrating the Pacific into global civilization (Mechnikov, 2013: 202). Thirdly, the Indian Ocean evolved alongside the progress of civilization, expanding from coastal inland seas to encompass all inhabited regions of the globe over time (Mechnikov, 2013: 203). Water, according to Mechnikov, not only influences geological phenomena and plant life but also shapes the history of animals and humanity by encourag-ing civilizations to migrate from river basins and valleys to coastal shores and beyond. Mechnikov categorizes these historical periods succinctly:

1. **The Ancient Ages (River Period)**
    *   Origins of the four great ancient civilizations (Egypt, Mesopotamia, India, and China) in river basins.
    *   Era of isolated peoples, ended by the 18th century.
    *   Early international relations began with conflicts between Egypt and Assyria-Babylonia, culminating in the Phoenician federations around 800 years before the Christian Era.
2. **The Middle Ages (Mediterranean Period)**
    *   Mediterranean Sea era: Dominated by oligarchic states like Phoenicia, Carthage, Greece, and Rome, up to Constantine the Great.
    *   Maritime era: Starting with the establishment of Constantinople (Byzantium), expanding the influence to the Black Sea and subse-quently the Baltic throughout the medieval period.
3. **The Modern Era or Oceanic Period**
    *   Atlantic era: From the discovery of America through the "gold fever" in California and Alaska, the rise of English influence in Australia, Russian colonization along the Amur River, and the opening of China and Japan to European influence.

- World epoch: This contemporary era of civilization, marked prominently by internationalism, signifies a phase where global interactions, the association of peoples, and the rights of individuals, particularly began with the Declaration of the Rights of Man and of Citizens.

These classifications by Mechnikov provide a comprehensive framework illustrating the evolution of human civilization through dynamic interactions with the world's oceans and seas across different historical epochs, while his emphasis on environmental factors over racial theories represented a more progressive approach for his time.

Conclusion

In this chapter, the author has delved into Mechnikov's comprehensive theory of civilization's development, emphasizing the central role of cooperation over geographic determinism. Mechnikov's approach presents a significant departure from theories that attribute societal progress primarily to environmental factors or racial hierarchies. Instead, he posits that the essence of civilization's growth lies in human interactions with nature and, more critically, in the ability of people to collaborate and achieve solidarity.

Mechnikov argued that there is only one fundamental law of societal development: "the law of cooperation." He believed that the reasons for the emergence and evolution of civilizations and corresponding social institutions need to be sought not solely in the geographical environment but in humanity's interactions with nature, more specifically, in the ability of people to cooperate and achieve solidarity. For Mechnikov, the progressive course of human societies is characterized by cooperation, which is immeasurably more complex than the life and activity of animals and plants. He posited that it is not merely the presence of a river that creates civilization, but the cooperation required to utilize it effectively. This need for coordination, stimulated by geographical challenges, drives collective organization. Thus, Mechnikov assigns significant importance to "the great historical rivers" as catalysts for social cooperation and progress.

Mechnikov's theory emphasizes the dynamic and multifaceted nature of human societies, which evolve through cooperative efforts rather than being solely shaped by their physical environment. His analysis of ancient civilizations, particularly those that flourished along significant rivers such as the Nile, Tigris, Euphrates, Indus, and Yellow River, illustrates how environmental challenges necessitated collective action and innovation. These civilizations, according to Mechnikov, did not rise to prominence merely because of their favourable geographical settings but because of the social structures and cooperative behaviours they developed in response to their environments.

By examining the historical epochs rooted in the basins of significant rivers, Mechnikov underscores the transformative power of human collaboration. He categorizes the development of civilizations into three distinct phases: the river age, the maritime era, and the oceanic era. This progression highlights how human societies have continually adapted to and transcended their geographical constraints through cooperative endeavours, leading to increasingly complex and interconnected civilizations.

Mechnikov also challenged the deterministic views of his contemporaries, who attributed civilization's progress to racial superiority or simple environmental determinism. He argued that such perspectives overlook the profound impact of socio-economic and environmental conditions in shaping human history. Mechnikov's emphasis on the role of collective action and environmental adaptation offers a more inclusive and nuanced understanding of civilization's evolution, recognizing the contributions of diverse groups and contexts whilst rejecting the pseudoscientific racial hierarchies prevalent in his era.

Significantly, Mechnikov's intellectual journey represents an evolution from purely sociological concerns to a more integrated geographical-sociological approach. His early anarchist writings focused primarily on social organisation and the critique of authority, but his experience in Japan during the Meiji Restoration and his subsequent geographical studies led him to develop a more sophisticated understanding of how environmental factors interact with social cooperation. This synthesis allowed him to propose that whilst geography provides the stage, it is human cooperation that writes the script of civilisation.

Mechnikov's theory of cooperation provides a compelling framework for understanding the development of human societies that remains relevant today. His emphasis on solidarity and collective action resonates with contemporary challenges such as climate change, global inequality, and international cooperation. By focusing on the interactions between humans and their environment, and the essential role of cooperation, Mechnikov presents a holistic view of civilization's growth that anticipates modern theories of sustainable development and social resilience.

However, it is important to acknowledge the limitations of Mechnikov's approach. His geographical determinism, whilst more nuanced than that of his contemporaries, still tends to oversimplify the complex factors that contribute to societal development. Modern scholarship recognises that cultural, technological, political, and economic factors play equally important roles in shaping civilisations. Additionally, while Mechnikov challenged racial theories of his time, his work still reflects some of the Eurocentric biases typical of 19th-century scholarship.

In conclusion, Mechnikov's integration of sociological and geographical thought offers valuable insights into the development of human civilisation.

His "law of cooperation" provides an alternative to both environmental determinism and social Darwinism, emphasising instead the creative potential of human solidarity in response to environmental challenges. This perspective not only enriches our understanding of historical development but also underscores the importance of solidarity and collective effort in addressing contemporary global challenges. Through this lens, we can appreciate the intricate web of factors that have shaped human civilization and continue to influence our shared future. Mechnikov's work reminds us that progress emerges not from competition or favourable circumstances alone, but from the fundamental human capacity to cooperate, adapt, and build solidarity across diverse communities and challenging environments. As we face unprecedented global challenges today, his emphasis on cooperation over competition offers a valuable framework for understanding how societies can successfully navigate complex environmental and social transformations.

Note

1. Lev Ilyich Mechnikov's work was first published in French as La Civilisation et les grands fleuves historiques (1889) and later translated into Russian as Tsivilizatsiya i velikie istoricheskie reki (Ajris-Press, 2013). In English, the title would be Civilization and the Great Historical Rivers.

Bibliography

Andreev, F. M. (2019). A Son of Kharkiv Soil and his Double Anniversary. *Accents and Paradoxes of Modern Philology, 1*(4), 7–25.
Bakunin, M. A. (1970). *God and the State* (1st ed.). Dover Publications.
Darwin, Charles. 1958. The Origin of Species. Signet.
Konishi, S. (2013). *Anarchist Modernity: Corporatism and Japanese-Russian Intellectual Relations in Modern Japan.* Harvard University Asia Center.
Kropotkin, P. (1989). *Mutual Aid: A Factor of Evolution* (1st ed.). Black Rose Books.
Mechnikov, L. (1881). *L'empire Japonais.* Imp. orientale de L'Atsume Gusa.
Mechnikov, L. (1886). Revolution and Evolution. *The Contemporary Review, 50,* 412–437.
Mechnikov, L. (2013). *Tsivilizatsiya i velikie istoricheskie reki.* Ajris-Press.
Spencer, H. (2019). *The Principles of Biology; Volume 1.* Wentworth Press.
Turner, J. H., & McCaffree, K. (2021). Evolutionary Theorizing in Sociology's Formative Period: Implications for Theorizing Today. In S. Abrutyn & O. Lizardo (Eds.), *Handbook of Classical Sociological Theory* (pp. 65–90). Springer International Publishing. https://doi.org/10.1007/978-3-030-78205-4
White, J. D. (1976). Despotism and Anarchy: The Sociological Thought of L. I. Mechnikov. *The Slavonic and East European Review, 54*(3), 395–411. https://www.jstor.org/stable/4207300?seq=1

2

MIKHAIL ALEKSANDROVICH BAKUNIN

A life of theory, a life of praxis

Deirdre Ruscitti Harshman

In an edited volume designed to show how intellectual movements within the Russian Empire formed a budding network of sociological thought and theory, the inclusion of Mikhail Aleksandrovich Bakunin (1814–1876) may seem a bit odd. Bakunin's influence on social theory is certainly clear: as one of the most prominent anarchist activists and thinkers of the nineteenth century, his work would leave an undeniable mark on the field of radical politics, as well as in the growing academic discipline of sociology. But his relationship to the Russian Empire—the subject of this volume's scholarly intervention—is less discussed. As a politically radical thinker and activist, Bakunin left the Russian Empire at the age of 26 in 1840; he would only return involuntarily under imprisonment and internal exile from 1851 to 1861, before escaping to live the rest of his life abroad. Although his work would find supporters in the Russian Empire, it remained arguably more popular and more well-known outside of its borders (Pyziur 1955: 4). Despite the geographical range of his travels and influence, however, Bakunin's anarchist theory emerged in large part out of a reaction against the political and social structure of the Russian Empire. Although Bakunin would do most of his work outside of the confines of the Russian imperial state, its anatomy had an indelible impact on his entire body of work. In particular, Bakunin's emphasis on the concept of radical freedom—a core tenant of his vein of anarchist thought—illustrates just how the stultifying limitations of the tsarist state encouraged radical thinkers like Bakunin to expand far beyond them.

This chapter moves roughly chronologically through Bakunin's life, examining his work against the backdrop of how it challenged the norms

DOI: 10.4324/9781003541004-3

and expectations of the Imperial Russian state and society. This juxtaposition is not meant to postulate a simple antagonistic relationship between the two factors (i.e. that Bakunin formulated his theories and practices directly in opposition to the Russian Empire), least of all because authorial intent is difficult to ascribe. Nonetheless, by holding the two in parallel, it is possible to explore how the path of Bakunin's work increasingly built a vision of the world that was, in many ways, directly antithetical to the imperial state. Whereas the Russian Empire in the mid-nineteenth century prioritized autocracy, hierarchy, and patriarchy, Bakunin became a fierce advocate for communalism, free association, and radical equity. Such a marked contrast caused Soviet historian Yuri Steklov to go so far as to position Bakunin as "the founder not only of European anarchism, but also of Russian populist rebellionism, and therefore of Russian Social Democracy, from which the Communist Party emerged" (Pyziur 1955: 14).

To trace how Bakunin's theory and actions developed and shifted throughout his life, this chapter is subdivided into three sections. The first section contextualizes the Bakunin family's position within the hierarchy of the Russian Empire and explains how the young Mikhail Aleksandrovich Bakunin's early philosophies were built on a deep antipathy towards the structure and practice of the imperial state. Through this antipathy, Bakunin began to build towards several of the key concepts that would define his later work, especially on the theme of radical freedom. This work would be cut short when Bakunin was arrested for his participation in an unsuccessful revolutionary movement in 1849; his resultant imprisonment and exile in the Russian Empire would last for over a decade. The second section traces what follows Bakunin's escape from exile and return to political activism, a period when Bakunin began to refine his theoretical framework. These efforts would include several key elucidations of Bakunin's revolutionary anarchism (including, most notably, Bakunin's theory of social revolution), as well as growing attempts to work with other major revolutionary theorists to build a more cohesive leftist movement through the First International. Such cooperative efforts would be ultimately unsuccessful, culminating in his expulsion from, and the collapse of, the First International. In the wake of this fallout, Bakunin would author several works that remain among his most well-known. The final section of this chapter examines these works, which are the most complete elucidation of Bakunin's anarchism and which advocated for a practice-driven, bottom-up view of revolutionary theory. Throughout his career—from his earliest works published under pseudonyms to his last major work of theory—the Russian Empire and its particular types of hierarchy and violence—remained central to how Bakunin defined what he struggled against.

Section 1: radical freedom

Like most politically active individuals in the nineteenth century Russian Empire, Mikhail Aleksandrovich Bakunin's introduction to politics began at home. The Russian autocratic system was such that it attempted to monopolize all political activity within the space of the court, through what the historian Richard Wortman called "reciprocal processes." In such processes, the practice of absolute rule was used to create the image of a transcendent monarch; such an image of transcendence was then used by the monarch to claim absolutist rule. Essentially, the system was designed to function as a sort of tautological loop (Wortman 1995: introduction). Although there were outright challenges to imperial power—the Pugachev Uprising and Decembrist Revolt are the two most prominent examples that precede Bakunin's life and show how mass discontentment arose from both the lower and upper estates, respectively—much of the frustration and desire for transformation was sublimated into more discrete political activity. Throughout the reign of Nikolai I (r. 1825–1855), politically engaged individuals began to meet in private residences to discuss and debate issues of the day. As the historian John Randolph has argued, the transformation of domestic space into a political sphere was not one of withdrawal or alienation from Russian society, but an assertive effort: "a privatization of the power and charisma heretofore associated with the imperial court" (Randolph 2007: 9). Such spaces marked the refusal to cede all political activity to the court itself, whilst simultaneously maintaining a critical voice in spite of repressive elements. One of the major hubs of such activity was the Bakunin family household, based out of Priamukhino in Tver' Province.

Mikhail Bakunin was the eldest son of Aleksandr Mikhailovich Bakunin (1768–1854) and Varvara Aleksandrovna Muravieva (1792–1864). Due to their shared progressive (but not radical) politics, both of his parents were interested in doing more than simply replicating the status quo, and they sought to create a home that would move beyond the rigid hierarchies that were typical in aristocratic households. When the two married, Aleksandr's letters emphasize that he saw his role as a partner, rather than a guardian (Randolph 2007: 99). Through their union, they worked to transform Priamukhino into a site open to those who might subtly—and perhaps even openly—to challenge social norms and expectations, with visits from some of the Decembrist leaders, the literary critic Vissarion Belinskii, and the poet Nikolai Stankevich, among others (Randolph: chapter 6). It was in this questioning environment that Mikhail Bakunin grew up, along with his ten siblings. Yet while the estate was undoubtedly more open to new ideas than the average noble household in early nineteenth-century Imperial Russia, social conventions still placed strong limitations on children, especially girls. Despite his heterodoxy, Aleksandr's re-imagining of what the domestic sphere could be was still built on a foundation of paternalism, and when the four Bakunin sisters—Liubov, Varvara, Tatiana, and Aleksandra—sought to move beyond the allowances set out by their father, tensions grew quickly. The oldest sister, Liubov, was locked into an unwanted engagement until her refusal to play along with a narrative of domestic bliss led to a massive argument and breakdown of the planned marriage. Throughout the engagement, Aleksandr displayed intense frustration at his children's lack of obedience—at one point, in his exasperation with Liubov, exclaiming, "Let her die, but let her fulfill her duties!" (Randolph 2007: 170). Perhaps it is not surprising that the novelist Ivan Turgunev—whose most famous work Fathers and Children (*Otsy i deti*, more commonly translated as Fathers and Sons) details the struggles of a family whose parents' push backs against some social boundaries end up dwarfed by their more radical children—was a guest of the household and a close personal relation to Tatiana Bakunina (Randolph 2007: chapter 5).

In addition to the particular dynamics of the Bakunin family, there were other elements of social restraint built into the imperial system surrounding young Mikhail Bakunin that he would have grown deeply familiar with. The most prominent of these would have been the institution of serfdom, a structural hierarchy that kept roughly half of the Russian Empire's peasant population chained to the land in a position of servitude. In 1814 (the year of Mikhail Bakunin's birth), 837 enserfed individuals were tied to the Bakunin estate in Priamukhino (Randolph 2007: 85). Although much of the state bureaucracy and many of Russia's noble families recognized the serfdom as a massive social injustice by the 1830s and 1840s, they were structurally unable to change it; autocracy meant that all changes had to come at the behest of the Tsar, a change Nikolai I refused to make (Lincoln 1986: 59, 107–109). Maintaining and enforcing this social system was of course another imperial institution: the Russian Army. At the age of fifteen, as was common among aristocratic families, Bakunin was trained at the Artillery School in the capital before being sent to serve as a junior officer in Poland shortly after the November Uprising (1830–1831) had been crushed. The experience, wrote his friend James Guillaume in a 1907 biography, "shocked the gently bred young officer and deepened his hatred of despotism" (Bakunin 1971: 23). As a young member of a noble household, the expectation was that participation in such systems would inculcate in Bakunin a sense of both responsibility and ownership, inducing a respect and appreciation for the mechanics of both internal and external empire.

Instead, Bakunin resigned from the Army after two years, left the family estate, and entered academia. At Moscow State University, Bakunin delved into philosophy, becoming a member of one of the budding student "circles" (*kruzhki*), led by Nikolai Stankevich on German Romanticism. As had been the case with Bakunin, Stankevich had also been pushed towards state and military service as a young nobleman, but similarly grew frustrated with their limitations and instead turned to academia in order to focus on "higher interests" (Randolph 2007: 175). Although Stankevich's circle focused on philosophical questions, Stankevich's approach encouraged young students to use these frameworks to re-conceptualize their own lives. In the words of John Randolph: "Stankevich helped his contemporaries translate the central ambitions of post-Kantian philosophy (self-knowledge, autonomy, and progressive agency in society) into compelling Russian terms, creating new norms, practices, and narratives for modern Russian manhood in particular" (Randolph 2007: 176). Interested in pursuing this path further, Bakunin travelled to Berlin to continue his education.

Bakunin arrived in Berlin in 1840, and his interest in political philosophy and its practical applications came with him. Bakunin's early interests centred around the concept of pan-Slavicism—specifically, in its application as a tool that could not only rally together those who had been oppressed by existing state structures but potentially permit them to overthrow the sociopolitical status quo. Even in his early years as an entrant into the realm of radical politics—subsequent biographers have regularly distinguished this period, from 1840 to his arrest in 1849, as preceding his explicitly anarchist politics—it is not difficult to see the development of several key concepts, most notably that of radical freedom, which would come to define Bakunin's work in the decades to come.

Bakunin's first major work of political significance, titled "The Reaction in Germany" (published in 1842 under the pseudonym Jules Elysard), opened with the assertion that a popular ache for radical freedom was at the core of the wave of revolutionary fervour that spread throughout Europe in the 1840s. "Freedom, the realization of freedom: who can deny that this is what today heads the agenda of history?" he asked in the opening salvo of the short essay (Bakunin 1971: 56). He would develop this theme throughout this essay, as well as in other short pieces authored throughout the 1840s and beyond, but at its core lay a few key arguments. Firstly, Bakunin asserted that this popular push for revolutionary freedom emerged in reaction to the repressive elements present within existing societies. The Russian Empire's repressive hierarchical structure, he argued, kept the nations within it "so long enslaved within its borders," (Bakunin 1971: 66–67) and made the term "Russian" synonymous with "slave and executioner" (Bakunin 1971: 59). Such a repressive system, Bakunin stated, could never have true popular support—any popular conception of the Tsar as a popular figure was a fiction. "No, gentleman, the Russian people are not happy!" he stated at a speech in Paris in 1847 (Bakunin 1971: 60). The goal of political and social revolution was to trigger that deep well of resentment and anger, and to use it as a tool to tear down these existing structures and institutions, and to lead to "the emancipation of sixty million men" across the Russian Empire (Bakunin 1971: 60).

These groundswells of popular support Bakunin saw as producing a self-perpetuating chain, with each revolutionary attempt sparking future events down the line (Bakunin 1971: 63). Such a vision of freedom—as a wave of radical actions sweeping across the land—became a core component of Bakunin's political philosophy. Rather than emanating from a set of prescriptive tenets, Bakunin saw radical change as a force unto itself. A successful mass movement of radical thought and action could be studied and understood—even augmented or adjusted—but the role of the political theorist was, ultimately, to recognize that such popular will was inevitably beyond any individual's control (Bakunin 1971: 56–57).

As mentioned earlier, Bakunin's early writings also relied on concepts that he would largely abandon in his later work: most notably, elements of pan-Slavic nationalism and on religious imagery. At the time, both were commonly wielded tools by the various revolutionary movements of the 1840s with which Bakunin identified, and so it is no surprise that they found their way into his theoretical synthesis. In these early works, Bakunin saw both communal ideologies as useful springboards toward political and social revolution, often using them bombastically in order to pull as many people into the fray as possible. "Repent, repent, the Kingdom of the Lord is at hand!" he wrote at the conclusion of a pamphlet from 1842. "Let us therefore trust the eternal Spirit which destroys and annihilates only because it is the unfathomable and eternal source of all life. The passion for destruction is a creative passion, too!" (Bakunin 1971: 57). Such elements would be discarded in later works, as Bakunin cites both nationalism and religion as examples of ideologies that reified the hierarchical worldview that his own work focused on dismantling.

Arguably the biggest influence for Bakunin's later work came not from his earlier writing but from what he was doing when he was not writing. "No theory, no ready-made system, no book that has even been written will save the world," he wrote on the subject in the 1840s. "I cleave to no system" (Carr 1937: 175). Such thought would form the basis of Bakunin's later opinions on political theory: useful, according to his 1873 work Statism and Anarchy, only so long as it emerged out of practice. It is therefore little surprise that a political theorist whose own philosophy highlighted the limitations of the profession would increasingly prioritize action; and amidst the revolutionary movements sweeping through the European continent at the time, he would get his chance.

As the revolutionary fervour rose to the fever pitch of 1848, Bakunin's personal involvement in radical movements took him to Frankfurt, Berlin,

Prague, Breslau, before finally ending in Chemnitz. It was during these travels that Bakunin drew personal inspiration from the major peasant rebellions in Russian history, particularly those led by Stepan Razin and Yemelyan Pugachev, which he described as "the first great protest of the rural population against its oppressors" (Carr 1937: 187). Summarizing the influence that Russia's peasant revolutions had had on him, Bakunin later wrote that every "living fruit of human progress [had been] watered with human blood" (Carr 1937: 187). It was this historical inspiration that directed not only Bakunin's political thought, but his actions as well. One of Bakunin's compatriots, Aleksandr Herzen, for example, described an incident in which Bakunin saw a group of German peasants demonstrating around a baron's castle; Bakunin went up to them and provided instructions on how to burn down the castle, a step the peasants took as Bakunin departed (Carr 1937: 188).

Bakunin's early work—both in writing and in practice—was put to a sudden (temporary) stop when he was captured in Chemnitz, then part of the Kingdom of Saxony. Bakunin had been a leading figure in the 1849 May Uprising, an attempt to overthrow the King of Saxony after the monarch had disbanded the recently formed national assembly, the Frankfurt Parliament. Bakunin was initially sentenced to death by the Saxon courts, but that sentence was commuted to life imprisonment at the behest of Russian Emperor Nikolai I—largely so he could be transferred into their custody. In 1851, Bakunin was returned to the Russian Empire and imprisoned, first in the Peter and Paul Fortress in St. Petersburg, then eventually transferred to Shlisselburg Fortress (Bakunin 1977).

While in the Peter and Paul Fortress, Bakunin wrote (at the personal behest of Nikolai I) an extensive and somewhat scattershot confession.—In perhaps its most famous passage, he wrote, "In Bohemia, I wanted a decisive radical revolution which would overthrow everything and turn everything upside down," adding later, "In short, the revolution I planned was terrible and unprecedented [...]" (Bakunin 1971: 69). Bakunin took time to reframe several of his actions to emphasize their destructive aspect, but also maintained that much of the destruction had been aimed primarily at property, not people. As a confessional document, Bakunin was also limited in any attempts at providing actual reasoning or justification for such destruction. To make matters worse, he began to suffer from scurvy and malnutrition while imprisoned, causing his teeth to fall out. Although interpreting these years is difficult to do with any certainty—anything clearly written under substantial duress should always be approached with a critical eye—it is not hard to see how these years and experiences would have reified and rigidified Bakunin's deep distrust and frustration at the structure of the Russian Empire. Bakunin's early orientation had been largely formed by objections to the strict hierarchies of the Russian Empire back when he was largely insulated from their worst effects as a member of an aristocratic family. Now, with his titles (and the protection they offered) stripped, the hierarchies and power plays at the heart of imperial politics likely seemed even more unfeeling and unforgiving.

Part of the reasoning behind the confession was to ask for some degree of clemency, in large part due to Bakunin's growing health problems. In 1857, Nikolai I's successor, Emperor Aleksandr II, commuted Bakunin's service to internal exile in the city of Tomsk, but within four years, Bakunin managed to escape whilst posing as a businessman. Heading east this time, he made his way to Japan before travelling across the Pacific to San Francisco, then across the North American continent to New York, and finally across the Atlantic Ocean before arriving in Liverpool—a global journey that took him all of five months. In a later letter sent to Herzen, Bakunin described feeling like he had "risen from the dead." It did not take long for his revolutionary work to resume (Wakayama 1978: 181–182).

Section 2: social revolution

In 1861, Bakunin completed his journey back to Europe and wasted little time reintegrating himself into the arena of radical politics. Over the next decade, Bakunin would work to outline his vision of the concept of social revolution.

At its core, Bakunin's concept of social revolution can be divided into two co-constitutive steps: the destruction of existing institutions and structures he considered to be limiting to human freedom, and the construction of new principles to guide a free society. Bakunin's 1866 work, "Revolutionary Catechism," was designed to outline the practical steps a movement could take to implement a social revolution: a process in which the excision of ideologies and frameworks that upheld and maintained existing hierarchies was absolutely fundamental (Bakunin 1971: 76–97). In particular, Bakunin targeted all forms of a centralized state (with particular attention paid to abolishing monarchical or autocratic systems); all state religions (or faiths that had a privileged position thanks to the state); all class and estate systems, as well as all forms of privileged ranks; all forms of centralized administration, including bureaucracies, standing armies, and state police; and all institutions where members had been appointed by the state, including many judiciaries and institutions of higher education (Bakunin 1971: 77–79). The utilitarian functions of these systems—if any –would be wholly replaced by means created through free communes or other organizations that had been born through bottom-up, democratic processes. The systematic dismantling of these institutions was so crucial, Bakunin asserted, because their continuation would make "the practical realization of freedom [...] forever impossible" (Bakunin 1971: 77).

Bakunin's understanding of the exclusionary and hierarchical nature central to these institutions' social and political functions, therefore, left him at odds with many of the trends emerging in the burgeoning study of sociology. Auguste Comte, for example—Bakunin's contemporary and one of the intellectual founders of the sociological discipline—similarly saw the contemporary world as in the process of shedding its old forms of social organization. To Comte, and many other sociologists, one of the key roles of academics and of the scientific process was to construct the new forms that would take their place—new institutions, structures, and hegemonies. In contrast, Bakunin questioned the very nature of these structures, arguing that any structure that upheld difference or ranking was itself inherently corruptive. Any hierarchical social or political system—even those designed to produce greater social equity—would be unable to do so as its very existence reinforced inequality. The only way to move beyond such limitations, Bakunin argued, was to build from the ground up, using methods of free association, guaranteed through a robust program of individual rights.

If hierarchical systems—even those designed with equitable intentions—were out of the question for Bakunin, then how would society be structured? To this end, Bakunin proposed that the basis of this new society be the "completely autonomous commune." These communes would be formed out of existing local communities, and they would give every adult in said community the ability to vote on every decision made. These communes would be able to decide whether they wanted to create voluntary federations with other communes, in order to form provinces; such provinces would then be able to voluntarily organize into federative nations. At each stage of the process, though, Bakunin emphasized the importance of voluntary participation: no commune would ever be forced to federate, and if communities found their participation in these federative provinces or nations to be unsatisfactory, they would be able to readily undo the federative bonds that tied them to other communes (Bakunin 1971: 83). From these varied federative communities would emerge more equitable bases for creating new social institutions, including judicial systems, sites of higher education, and any services that had previously been provided by state bureaucracies. They would also play a key role in defending the communes against any attempts to restore old hierarchical systems (Bakunin 1971: 78).

In order to protect these rights of free association, each individual would be guaranteed a robust program of individual rights. The most critical of these rights was that no limitations be placed on individual freedoms.

> The freedom of adults of both sexes must be absolute and complete, freedom to come and go, to voice all opinions, to be lazy or active, moral or immoral, in short, to dispose of one's person or possessions as one pleases, being accountable to no one.
>
> *(Bakunin 1971: 79)*

If an individual chose to affiliate with an autonomous commune, and if the members of that commune joined a federated province or nation, then all questions were to be settled with direct votes, governed by a practice of universal equal suffrage for all adults (Bakunin 1971: 80).

It is critical to note, however, that for Bakunin, theoretical contributions were always dwarfed by the practical; future models of social revolution were only useful insomuch as they could provide a path forward for action. However, the European revolutionary movement had been set back heavily from its 1848 heyday, and for now, rebuilding the movement itself was the most critical and pressing task. To that end, Bakunin began to become involved with a new effort: the International Workingmen's Association (better known by its later name, the First International, as it shall be henceforth referred to), an organization that aimed to bring together a variety of leftist and radical movements so that what had previously been disparate orientations would be able to work together effectively. Bakunin joined the movement in 1868, four years after its founding, and in a series of articles written for the French newspaper L'Égalité, he outlined his enthusiasm about being part of a broad working-class movement that could free labour activism from its ties to bourgeois society. He wrote shortly after joining in August 1869.

> Do you understand that faced with the formidable coalition of all the privileged classes, all the capitalists, and all the states, an isolated workers' association, local or national, even in one of the greatest European nations, can never triumph, and that faced with this coalition, victory can only be achieved by a union of all the national and international associations into a single universal association which is none other than the great International Workingmen's Association? ... Since all politics, as far as the emancipation is concerned, is infected with reactionary elements, the International had first to purge itself of all political systems, and then build upon the ruins of the bourgeois social order the new politics of the International.
>
> *(Bakunin 1971: 162 and 164)*

This was a tall order. When describing the First International, it is difficult to summarize even what its primary goal was, as its major contributors and members could never fully agree on what they wanted to achieve. While all of its contributors shared a dislike of the existing status quo of industrial capitalism propped up with state power, there were a myriad of highly divergent views on how to move beyond it; even more on what sort of new status quo should be created in its stead. Bakunin's own perspective was shaped most significantly by his viewpoint that all political power would be inherently corrupting, even to "sincere socialists and revolutionaries." Consolidating political power in any form, he believed, would lead to a consolidation of wealth, and together the two factors would inevitably lead to corruption (Maximov 1953: 358). To quote the prominent radical sociologist Alvin W. Gouldner: "In Bakunin's view, the struggle against the main concentration of power in society, the state, was no less necessary than the struggle against capital" (Gouldner 1982: 863). In marked contrast were Karl Marx and his followers (the most prominent faction of the First International). A guiding principle of Marx's vision, historical materialism, posited that the seizure of the means of production and the proletariat's control over surplus value would initiate a series of systematic, radical changes. In other words, consolidation of wealth and power in the hands of the working class lay at the heart of Marxist radicalism—exactly what Bakunin believed would fundamentally doom the whole project.

Despite Bakunin's (and others') hopes that the First International would be able to transcend the significant differences among leftist movements, it would ultimately fall victim to them. In 1871, writing about the Paris Commune, Bakunin outlined a stark difference in the approaches of the "revolutionary socialists" (with whom he aligned himself) and the "authoritarian communists," and posited that the two camps were largely irreconcilable (Bakunin 1971: 262). Relations deteriorated between Bakunin and the larger Marxist faction, and in 1872, Bakunin was expelled from the First International entirely. In the wake of this expulsion, Bakunin would spend the final years of his life more clearly elucidating his positions, most notably through two key works: God and the State and Statism and Anarchy.

Section 3: anarchism

By 1872, despite (or perhaps because of) his expulsion from the First International, Bakunin had emerged as a looming figure within the European revolutionary movement, almost akin to a living legend. Both contemporary and later biographies often highlight how much of Bakunin's reputation was bound up in his enthusiasm, energy and physicality. "Everything about him was colossal," said the German composer Richard Wagner, and fellow Russian revolutionary Alexander Herzen declared that Bakunin "was born not under an ordinary star but under a comet" (Bakunin 1971: xiii–xiv). Even in his older years, Bakunin continued to prioritize revolutionary action and contemporaneity over structuralist debates and long-term planning (Carr 1937: chapter 8). It is unsurprising, then, that Bakunin's written contribution to the revolutionary scene was lighter than some of his contemporaries. He had written several well-circulated works (most notably the Revolutionary Catechism of 1866), but Bakunin likely saw published theory as one tool in a revolutionaries' toolkit; rather than one's primary weapon. However, as it became increasingly clear that Bakunin's approach differed in key ways from his contemporaries—most famously, in regard to the rift from Marx and statist communism, but also in his split from his former close friend Sergei Nechaev over Nechaev's turn towards nihilistic violence—it is likely Bakunin would have wanted to more clearly outline his particular views. His first attempt was through an incomplete theoretical work titled *The Knouto-German Empire,* followed by a more practically-minded work titled *Statism and Anarchy.* Viewed together, they offer a comprehensive view of Bakunin's major contributions, much of it massively influential in establishing and defining the canon of European anarchist thought.

In the early 1870s, Bakunin began writing a piece that was intended to be his magnum opus. This work, to be titled *The Knouto-German Empire*, was intended to be a sprawling examination and critique of how multiple repressive structures and institutions worked in tandem. As the title suggests, the work focused on the two states with which Bakunin took the most umbrage, the Russian Empire (with Knouto in the title deriving from the Russian word for a whip) and the newly formed German Empire. As he had done with his earlier writings, Bakunin positioned the Russian and German states as a foil against which he could clarify his own arguments and positions. Although *The Knouto-German Empire* would never be completed—Bakunin died before he finished it—the second part of the work was discovered and published posthumously under the title God and the State in 1882 (Bakunin 1970: viii). The goal of God and the State was, in the words of historian Paul Avrich, a "repudiation of authority and coercion in all its forms" (Bakunin 1970: vii). The work introduced this concept through a combination of allegory and sociological analysis. It begins with the latter, as Bakunin opened the work by using a materialist viewpoint to explain how mankind evolved, noting that our species' progenitors were able to transcend the animalistic through two impulses: "the power to think and the desire to rebel" (Bakunin 1970: 9). These two factors not only distinguished the earliest examples of mankind from the animal world, Bakunin wrote, but they also gave humans the tools they needed to continue to evolve human society (Bakunin 1970: 12). Standing in the way, he argued, were those who used coercion, violence, social pressure, and other tools to try to disincentivize or otherwise limit free thought. Institutions like religion, he wrote, try to dissuade people from this natural inclination to change and grow, instead requiring people to "remain an eternal beast" (Bakunin 1970: 10). Those who are trapped under these systems are "reduced, intellectually and morally as well as materially, to the minimum of human existence, confined in their life like a prisoner in a prison, without horizons, without outlets…" (Bakunin 1970: 16). The only true escape from this trap, Bakunin suggested, was to break down these limiting systems through the process of social revolution. Indeed, Bakunin interpreted the current revolutionary upswing as an example of this longer process of change that he argued had defined mankind from its onset. "He [mankind] has gone out from animal slavery, and passing through divine slavery, a temporary condition between his animality and his humanity, he is now marching on the conquest and realization of human liberty," he wrote (Bakunin 1970: 21).

The process of breaking from these existing institutions, Bakunin acknowledged, was a difficult one. Institutions like the Russian Empire and the Catholic Church wanted to tamp down man's natural impulse to try to grow, but they were not alone. Drawing on the themes that had led to his fight over the First International, Bakunin added that new institutions, even those designed to be progressive, could have the same despotic impulse. Historians have speculated that the "German" in the title of the original work likely referred not only to the recently formed German imperial state (as well as its Russian counterpart) but also to Marx and his followers, for— as Bakunin wrote—both sought to assume control over the fate of ordinary people through the use of authority (Gouldner 1982: 857–858; Bakunin 1970: 28). "The government of science and of men of science, even be they positivists, disciples of Auguste Comte, or, again, disciples of the doctrinaire school of German Communism, cannot fail to be impotent, ridiculous, inhuman, cruel, oppressive, exploiting, maleficent," he wrote (Bakunin 1970: 55).

In late 1871, as the fight over the First International was on the verge of its apex, he put *The Knouto-German Empire* aside. When Bakunin returned to writing after the conclusion of the matter, he started a new work that would more clearly elucidate his views, especially in contrast to those with whom he had recently split. Thus, in *Statism and Anarchy* (Bakunin's last major work, written and published in 1873), perhaps the most dominant theme was a deep frustration with the revolutionary trend towards reliance on the state and its authority. "He who is given power will inevitably become an oppressor and exploiter of society," he cautioned (Bakunin 1971: 327). If the power dynamics behind a reformist or revolutionary government mirrored the patterns and tendencies of its predecessor, it would always replicate the same problems as its predecessor, Bakunin argued. "...[T]he people will feel no better if the stick with which they are being beaten is labelled 'the people's stick'" (Bakunin 1971: 338).

In contrast to statism, Bakunin set out to create a different revolutionary model, which he positioned as an evolution of Pierre-Joseph Proudhon's rejection of the state and championing of mutualist societies: anarchism. This was not the first time he had advocated for such an approach. In God and the State, Bakunin included a prominent section on how anarchist thought and practice were designed to push against entrenched institutions and advocate for social revolution.

In a word, we reject all legislation, all authority, and all privileged, licensed, official, and legal influence, even though arising from universal suffrage, convinced that it can turn only to the advantage of a dominant minority of exploiters against the interests of the immense majority in subjection to them," he wrote. "This is the sense in which we are really Anarchists.

(Bakunin 1970: 35)

In *Statism and Anarchy*, he noted that this rejection would always set anarchist thought apart from other sociological and political movements, as those other movements would always see the state as "the only salvation for society" (Bakunin 1971: 328). In contrast, Bakunin's vision of anarchism stripped away that reliance, leaving a model of society in which all power derives only "from the people themselves, an elemental force sweeping away all obstacles" (Bakunin 1971: 325).

Statism and Anarchy—the last major writing of Bakunin's life—concluded with a reflection on Russia. Although he had written extensively about how the Russian imperial state worked diligently to keep social revolution at bay, Bakunin also believed that one of the best hopes for producing such a change came from the Russian people themselves. Despite suffering in conditions of intense deliberate deprivation, isolated and atomized in small, disconnected villages, the Russian peasantry showed their desire for freedom through the constant flow of small revolts and uprisings. The best model for social revolution, he wrote, was to draw upon the examples of spontaneous peasant revolts that turned into mass affairs, like those led by Razin and Pugachev (Bakunin 1971: 348–349). The Russian imperial state may have provided the exact model of what Bakunin wanted to move away from, but the Russian people themselves were a source of inspiration.

Shortly after the publication of *Statism and Anarchy*, Bakunin retired from revolutionary work. Based on some of Bakunin's private letters from this period, the ageing radical's worldview in these final years of his life was heavily coloured by melancholy. "I am too old, too sick, and—shall I confess it?—too disillusioned, to participate in the work," he wrote in 1875 to his close friend, the geographer Jacques Élisée Reclus. He felt that the systems against which he had spent his life struggling had won the fight, at least for the time being. In the same letter to Reclus, these frustrations came through clearly. "Poor humanity! It is evident that it can extricate itself from this cesspool only by an immense social revolution. But how can this revolution come about?" he wrote. "[H]ow to organize them, when they do not even care enough about their own fate to know or put into effect the only measures that can save them?" (Bakunin 1971: 354–355). Indeed at the time of his death in 1876, the revolutionary struggles of which Bakunin had been a part still hung in a sort of liminal space: driven by a growth in discontentment with the status quo, but deeply fractured and ultimately ineffective. As his comments suggested, the struggle would continue for some time.

In the decades of continuing struggles between systems of social and political power, and the people who live within/under them, Bakunin's perspective on revolution has held a powerful—though often marginalized—sway in the annals of social revolution. As Bakunin predicted, the appeal of a state apparatus—even to fellow leftist revolutionaries—has remained a stumbling block towards the true "from below" social movements he called for. Indeed, many have struggled with envisioning life beyond the state, viewing Bakunin's calls for active and ongoing mass social revolutions as unworkable and purely theoretical. But as evident from his writings and personal experiences, Bakunin saw great value in the history of the world around him; in the revolutionary spirit of those around him; and in the work he and other revolutionaries were doing—not toward a well-defined and structured society of the future, but simply toward a better present. To comprehend Bakunin's writing best one must understand the context in which he lived and wrote; to apply Bakunin best, one must understand the society in which one lives—and the work which must be done.

References

Bakunin, M. A. (1970). *God and the State*. Dover Publications.
Bakunin, M. A. (1971). *Bakunin on Anarchy*. Vintage Books.
Bakunin, M. A. (1977). *The Confession of Mikhail Bakunin*. Cornell University Press.
Carr, E. H. (1937). *Michael Bakunin*. Vintage Books.
Gouldner, Alvin (1982). Marx's Last Battle: Bakunin and the First International. *Theory and Society,* Vol. 11, No. 6, pp. 853–884.
Lincoln, Bruce (1986). *In the Vanguard of Reform: Russia's Enlightened Bureaucrats, 1825–1861*. Northern Illinois University Press.
Maximov, G. P. (1953). *The Political Philosophy of Bakunin*. The Free Press.
Pyziur, Eugene (1955). *The Doctrine of Anarchism*. The Marquette University Press.
Randolph, John (2007). *The House in the Garden: The Bakunin Family and the Romance of Russian Idealism*. Cornell University Press.
Wakayama, Kenji (1978). *Bakunin to Hakodate*. Yokohama, Kanagawa: Warera.
Wortman, Richard (1995). *Scenarios of Power: Myth and Ceremony in Russian Monarchy*. Princeton University Press.

3

ALEXANDER STRONIN

Foundations of Russian Political Sociology

Md Reza Habib

Introduction

Naturalism was an early component of sociology's development, just like positivism. Ideas such as organicism, social Darwinism, and geographical determinism represented the naturalistic method of studying society in foreign sociology, commonly referred to as "sociological naturalism" in Russia. The 1860s and 1870s were characterized by an organic trend in Russian sociology. Organicism was only one example of "sociological naturalism," which also encompassed any efforts to directly link social life to the natural world and interpret it using natural laws. Comparing nature and society through analogy was the primary cognitive strategy. Naturalism maintains that we should only study social processes in their natural environments. The scientific study of art and literature applied a similar form of naturalism. Many antipositivists argue that qualitative distinctions make natural science investigative methods ineffective for describing social issues. Naturalism, in this sense, excludes scientism. Naturalism and scientism are still prevalent in certain major sociology departments, including Chicago and McGill. The organicist school believed that the fundamental principles of growth and progress are universally applicable to both living nature and human societies. The three components of Russian organicism are the organic, mechanical, and geographical schools. Sociologists like Lilienfeld-Toal and Novikov belong to the first school, Stronin created the second, and Mechnikov led the third.

Within this field, A. I. Stronin was a pioneering thinker in Russia who helped establish sociology as a discipline, as well as its conceptual and categorical framework and methodological explanation. He also made

DOI: 10.4324/9781003541004-4

statements about the social function of the intelligentsia, the future structure of society, and the role of knowledge and information in new social conditions, all of which are extremely pertinent today. His ideas about the unity of the biological and the social, as well as the harmony in relationships between individuals and elements of society, are also very relevant.

Stronin, one of Russia's best-known sociological naturalists, applied the idea of an organic method to the study of society (Nemeth, 2018). The popularity of naturalistic theories has modified his legacy. Note that Stronin's work emerged simultaneously with Herbert Spencer's initial writings, emphasizing the issue of society's organic structure. Stronin, through his own reasoning and the passionate contradiction of a powerful and creative intellect, ultimately arrived at the same organic idea (Valerievna, 2006). He laid the essential foundations of his sociological perspective in his first publication, "History and Method." He is essentially a positivist and an adherent of Auguste Comte, as seen in this and other publications.

Some aspects of Stronin's work and sociological concepts were explored, analyzed, and studied by contemporary researchers. However, when considering some of the achievements of the Russian researcher's socio-philosophical and sociological heritage, it is obvious that Stronin's sociological ideas are currently underexplored in terms of their integrity and complexity. Both pre-revolutionary and contemporary Russian literature only took into account certain aspects of creativity, which is insufficient for a holistic understanding of the Russian sociological discipline. Additionally, the current task of Russian sociology involves identifying the most important and pressing social issues and devising logical solutions. It seems impossible to achieve these objectives without considering sociological science's classical past, examining and critically generalizing its experience, and taking into account new realities. So it makes perfect sense to look to the legacy of Russian sociologists from the late 19th and early 20th centuries. As a result, studying Stronin's works is reasonable and essential to build on the solid foundation of Russian sociological thought (Valerievna, 2006). Stronin's legacy as an organicist sociologist has been influenced by a heightened interest in naturalistic theories, particularly organicism. Now we can methodically and impartially analyze his worldview, and his complete ideological legacy, and assess his position in the history of intellectual thinking.

Biography of A. I. Stronin

In the 19th century, Alexander Ivanovich Stronin (1826–1889) was a renowned Russian philosopher, sociologist, publicist, writer, and teacher. He was born on February 20, 1826, in the hamlet of the Hotmysh district of Kursk province, and passed away on January 29, 1889, in Yalta. His father was a simple serf who excelled in his field and served as the primary treasurer of Prince Yusupov's Rakitinsky board. Stronin started attending the Priluksky district school when he was seven years old. Between 1837 and 1844, he was a student at the second Kyiv gymnasium, after which he enrolled in the law faculty at Kyiv University. However, after one year, he switched to the historical and philological department of the philosophical faculty and successfully obtained a candidate's degree in 1848 (Brockhaus & Efron, 1890; Parhomenco, 2012).

Stronin taught at several gymnasiums for a while before moving to the Poltava gymnasium in 1855, where he spent the next seven years and built an outstanding reputation in pedagogy. Stronin actively participated in the Sunday schools for the residents of Poltava. He even wrote and published a special textbook titled "ABC for Poltava Sunday School," (Stronin, 1861) in which he included a curriculum on literature and the natural sciences. Along with other teachers, he actively participated in opening a women's gym in Poltava and volunteered to teach there for free (Brockhaus & Efron, 1890; Matyushenko & Samsonova, 2014). During this period, Stronin became involved in political activity. He served as the "Land and Freedom" secret organization's representative in Poltava. The Minister of Public Education dismissed him from his job on June 24, 1862, and detained him on September 3, 1862 "for disseminating obscene writings and brochures." His involvement with literacy organizations, Sunday schools, committees for setting up public libraries and lectures, and plans to launch a newspaper were all interpreted as evidence of Little Russia's separatist propaganda (Brockhaus & Efron, 1890; Matyushenko & Samsonova, 2014).

In 1858, Stronin visited Herzen in London and promoted his writings there. In 1862, authorities detained him and housed him at the Peter and Paul Fortress for several months (September to December), but they did not put him on trial due to a lack of evidence. He began studying philosophy and social studies in the Arkhangelsk area after his transfer in 1863. He worked in the district courts of Shenkursk (1867–1877), Arkhangelsk (1867–1868), and Pinega (1863–1866) (from May 1867). He co-authored the "Reference Book of the Arkhangelsk Province" in 1868 on the governor's behalf with P. S. Efimenko (Brockhaus & Efron, 1890; Matyushenko & Samsonova, 2014).

After leaving exile, he went to Petersburg. From November 30, 1869 until July 13, 1873 he worked under state control, and from August 3, 1871 to July 13, 1873 he was a St. Petersburg Judicial District sworn attorney. On June 27, 1873 the Vitebsk province appointed him as a justice of the peace in the Lepel district, and on March 3, 1876 they transferred him to the Lublin province to serve as the chairman of the Congress of Justices of the Peace in the first district. In 1877, they sent Stronin to the Ministry of Railways, where he became the ministry's legal counsel on May 1. On April

1, 1879 they promoted him to the position of acting. On January 16, 1887 he resigned from his position as a legal adviser to become a member of the Ministry of Railways' council. On October 4 of that year, he resigned due to illness. He then relocated to Yalta, where he passed away (Brockhaus & Efron, 1890; Matyushenko & Samsonova, 2014). In a broad sense, these are external events in Stronin's life, he was once accused of committing state crimes while also climbing to various official positions and making significant contributions to the research and development of education, politics, and society through his writings. Stronin was one of the first sociologists to analyze society as a series of interconnected factors that depend on and influence each other and find strategies to achieve social equilibrium. He used the biological organism analogy to structure society into classes, groups, and strata.

Scientific and literary contributions of Stronin

Stronin has made a variety of contributions to history, politics, social structure, and policy, including natural science. His major three works, "History and Method (1869)," "Politics as Science (1872)," and "Public History (1885)," made him famous in social science. They are three volumes of a single sociological treatise and, as such, they tell the stories of the method and overarching principles, the structure of society, and the development of society. However, Stronin's "Theory of Personality," a historical and philosophical manuscript, appears in his Imperial Public Library diary (Brockhaus & Efron, 1890; Akmalova et al., 2011).

Stronin also published some newspaper and magazine articles, all are published as a supplement to those. Some of his major articles, namely Circular October 19, (1870), Classicism and Realism (1871), Theory of Evidence (1872), Judicial Reform in the Kingdom of Poland (1876), Polish Crisis (1877), Innovator in Journalism (1877), Status in Status (1879), The Cause of Radicalism" (1879), Center and Outskirts (1882), Central and Provincial Press (1882), Colony and metropolis (1884), Judicial error (1885), and so on. In addition, in the Nordische Presse (1870, No. 256) S. published in German the article "Development of the Crisis in France" (Brockhaus & Efron, 1890).

In 1870, he published two brochures titled "France or Germany?" and "Peace or War," followed by "Anecdotal History of the Current War" (1877), which compiled the most influential letters about the war. In 1886, he published "Byron in Aleko's Translations," a collection of his own translations of Byron's poems. His translations are superb and capture the meaning of the well-known English poet, and they stand out for their clarity in thought transfer, figurativeness, and extraordinary conciseness of the poetry; the book is divided into four headings: "Jewish melodies," "Napoleon according to Byron," "family poems," and "Byronism as a form." His popular book on natural science, published under the pseudonym "Ivanov," sold ten thousand copies (Brockhaus & Efron, 1890; Akmalova et al., 2011).

In 1902, the author published the seventh edition of his "Tales of the Earth and Sky," capturing the story so vividly that it resonated throughout the village. Four other brochures for the people—"Stories about the Forces of the Earth," "Stories about the Life of the Earth," "Stories about Human Life," and "Stories about the Kingdom of Bova the King"—were published in the 1902 second edition. The Imperial Public Library housed Stronin's diary from the time he joined the service in 1848 until his death (Brockhaus & Efron, 1890; Akmalova et al., 2011).

Stronin's reputation as a sociologist is largely based on his three major publications: History and Method (St. Petersburg, 1869), Politics as a Science (St. Petersburg, 1872), and Public History (St. Petersburg, 1885). These three works cover the entirety of sociology and serve as a comprehensive treatise on this science. The three sections focus on the method and general principles, the structure of society, and the development of society. Despite strong criticism from N. K. Mikhailovsky, E. V. de Roberti, P. N. Tkachev, V. D. Spasovich, D. L. Mordovtsev, N. I. Kareev, and others, Stronin believed it was important to develop social knowledge in the image of the natural sciences, particularly biology. He believed that society is a single organism, and public institutions are merely different parts of that organism. It is hardly surprising that he believed sociology must already be akin to physiology (Stronin, 1872).

Stronin adhered to positivism in all of his scientific research. He founded his social theory to merge humanities and natural science knowledge to create a research process applicable to all sciences, if not universal. Stronin argued that new forms of scientific study were required after analyzing modern science's deductive and inductive procedures. He presents his classification of these methods, highlighting three forms of induction: evidence, based on obviousness; attentics, built not on external feelings but on the inner alone, not on experience and observation but on attention; and experimentalism, based on experience. He also highlights three forms of deduction: analytics (as a deduction of completion), dialectics (as a deduction of initiation), and hypotheses (as a deduction of production). Stronin believes that only experimentalism (from inductive forms) and hypotheses (from deductive ones) can be relevant for social science, but only in a transformed form, new forms. Among these many types (which he articulated in very explicit language), he singled out analogy (Nemeth, 2018). According to Stronin, the analogical methods used in the majority of natural sciences are a unique type of deduction that is applicable in social science. He also noted that the law of analogy is directly related to the proximity of the subjects of scientific investigation (Stronin, 1869). Stronin developed four laws of analogy: the law of the greatest affinity of phenomena or laws, the law of concentric affinity, the law of vertical affinity, and the law of horizontal affinity.

Stronin proposed the "dialectical isolation" method for the investigation of social phenomena. The core of this method was to absolutize specific aspects of reality and break them down into their parts. "Dialectical isolation" is a method of forming abstract concepts. According to Stronin, the formation of abstract ideal concepts through the method of dialectical isolation is not a goal but rather a means of scientific knowledge of the phenomenon itself, its characteristic qualities, and its properties. He implemented it as a procedure for creating ideal types, and it found widespread use in philosophical systems. Later, with M. Weber, it would become one of the primary sociological knowledge tools.

Stronin, for instance, claims that power tends towards unending expansion, rigidity, and violence without limitations if we isolate the concept of power or take power as such. Dialectics makes the essence of this social element transparent, a feat we cannot fully accomplish in society. Ego helps us fully comprehend the essence of the element.

Stronin also created another element of Russian sociological theory, albeit one that is less commonly used: the mechanical direction. He held that society abides by the principles of science, mathematics, and mechanics. He constructed a social model based on a geometric figure—the pyramid, in his opinion. The principles of physics and mechanics are followed by processes. Stronin began with the mechanical theory of society to analyze social structure. According to this theory, the structure of a society of a higher order, i.e., a state, is purely pyramidal with a pointed end or supreme power concentrated in one person, with an upper small tetrahedron inhabited by "owners of nature" (owners of the forces of nature), from which legislators and judges come out, etc., the middle spherical trapezoid—the bourgeoisie, which owns capital—and the lower broad base—the proletariat (owners of living muscular strength). According to him, society is entirely pyramidal in structure: the law of mechanics dictates that the body must turn in the direction of movement with its smallest surface for the most practical dissection of a traversed medium, and geometry recognizes no other figure than a pyramid to provide the body with the smallest or most pointed surface. However, the rules of physics state that an item cannot be stable if its base is not broad and unyielding. After carefully examining society's vertical structure, which the laws of mechanics dictate is necessary, Stronin discovers that the horizontal structure is circular; he even sketches a diagram of this universal mechanism, which, in addition to geometric considerations, is also physical because shifting the centre of gravity to the periphery threatens to upset the balance. His circular theory of society allows for the concurrent membership of numerous social unions, including concentric circles such as the family, community, and state.

According to the general biological law, Stronin distinguishes three major stages in the history of society's development: progress, which involves growth and body composition; stagnation, which balances addition and deconstruction; and regression, which involves decomposition. The movement from the physical to the mental, the bodily to the spiritual, the instinctive to the rational, the objective to the subjective, the immovable to the mobile, and "in general, from the animal to the human" were his interpretations of what it means to advance. In his view, the absence of new ideals and a delay in meeting new needs both contribute to the transition from progress to stagnation. As a supporter of the theory of cyclical development, Stronin characterizes the "death" of society as the start of a new cycle. According to general sociological law, social structures develop over a multilevel cycle in the direction of complication and differentiation. Stronin almost entirely shifts to a psychological perspective in his study of general political law. According to Stronin, "all politics starts from the psychological phenomenon of impression and reflex (deriving from this the general law of impression and reflex). According to this law, without impression and without reflex there is no moral life, and, conversely, any moral life consists of a long series of impressions and reflexes. The same is true in society, but only on a larger scale: impression and reflex are here nothing other than the action of the moral environment on the moral organism and the effect of this organism on this environment" (1872, p. 204). Stronin derives two essential principles from this law: the principle of interaction between the environment and the organism, as well as the principle of balance and harmony. This law and its principles express the active nature of politics. His works "Politics as a Science" and "Public History" demonstrate this trend, as the author, emulating Comte, seeks scientific methods to govern political life. Given that the focus of political sociology as a science is "active existence," which possesses both contemplative and aesthetic qualities, he divides it into three distinct policies: the policy of theoretical activity, the policy of aesthetic activity, and the policy of practice (Stronin, 1872).

According to general political law, social change occurs as a result of society's interaction with the environment. Stronin introduced the terms "incorporation" and "excorporation" to describe the process of examining the interaction of innovations with society's structure, as well as the extraction of non-functional parts from society. According to Stronin, society has three distinct political organs: the intelligentsia for contemplative life, the government for aesthetic life, and citizenship for active life. The common function among all of them is political creativity, with the specific functions being creativity, implementation, and embodiment. According to him, "the intelligentsia of society" includes all thinking people, the bearers of knowledge, and the organ of political development. However, in this structure, the intelligentsia, which fills the cone from bottom to top, and then from top to bottom, has a specific position for itself. It primarily functions as a political class because it is a proactive and active class. It serves as an engine in the larger social process. Stronin believed it to be a social force that could consciously advance society by steering its contradictory and complex movements. Thinkers, artists, and politicians comprised Stronin's division of the intelligentsia by profession. According to him, the government is an aesthetic public organ between the original intelligentsia and the final citizenship. A mediator between thought and legislation, intelligentsia and citizenship, the government coordinates the cerebellum movement. Stronin divides the government into three sub-organs: legislation, court, and administration. All three of these sub-organs deal with law; their functions are lawmaking, justice, and governance. Stronin concludes "Politics as a Science" with a theory of citizenship, which he refers to as "the private law of citizenship." The intelligentsia, with the assistance of government apparatuses, primarily establishes citizenship as a physical and economic force, not a political one. Stronin notes:

> In the broadest sense, citizens are all residents of the state, all members of civil society, not excluding even women or children..."Citizenship is a political echo of economic classes in the average sense, i.e., all those residents of the state who, apart from citizenship, have no other political role."
>
> *(Stronin, 1872, pp. 303–304)*

Stronin, on the other hand, divides "public" into its "elements" and describes the method by which each element evolved, comparing facts from the history of all epochs, peoples, and civilizations because, in his opinion, each element has its own evolution. In his last work, the "History of the Public" (1885), Stronin drew attention to the importance of studying the psychological aspects of social relations. In his assessment of "History of the Public," Kareev noted that the author of the book develops the views of Comte, Bockle, Littre, and Spencer, and that the book is a sociological attempt to treat historical progress. In his book, "History of the Public," he aimed to transform the factual history of community life into a theoretical framework, explaining the relationship between facts not through theological or philosophical perspectives but through scientific principles inherent in social life.

In his work "Theory of Personality," Stronin, the classic of Russian sociology, studied personality's aspiration to cognition and self-perfection.

In his historical-philosophical and sociological work, "The Theory of Personality," Stronin expresses positivistic views. The original manuscript of "The Theory of Personality" was kept by Stronin in the Russian National Library's Manuscript Department. The archivists date the manuscript to 1870. Stronin describes this work in his diary entries considerably later, in 1883. The original document spans five notebooks. Stronin's book exposes the "program of personality's theory," which is derived from the "philosophy of past," "philosophy of present," and "philosophy of future" (Stronin, 2013, pp. 132–176).

In our analysis of Stronin's theories on personality, we focus on its ethical, sociological, psychological, socio-pedagogical, and socio-psychological dimensions.

The sociological aspect of the study of personality is revealed through a series of factors:

a) An analysis of the factors and conditions necessary for successful self-education and socialization.
b) Mechanisms of social mobility;
c) Analyzing personal changes in the context of social mobility;
d) Analyzing the individual's egoism as a factor in their personal development;
e) The influence of the social environment on the character of the individual;
f) Establishing goals in an individual's life.
g) Influence of socioeconomic, legal, and other factors on the development of personal qualities.

According to Stronin, the following factors influence a person's socialization process: the laws of human nature, similar circumstances, the character's inherent conditions, natural education by society, artificial education by pedagogy and school, and, last but not least, among the artificial ones, self-education. All of these things inevitably influence a person against their will.

Stronin then demonstrates the limitations of the possibility of self-education: first, it cannot occur before the possibility of self-consciousness, i.e., when the character is already ready; second, it cannot occur otherwise than as the result of some extraneous impulse; third, it can only occur in general as an exceptional case and not as a custom of the majority; and fourth, it is impossible to influence oneself in the absence of knowledge and skills. All these requirements, of course, will result in the successful growth of the individual's self-education.

In this work, Stronin also dealt with the mechanism of social mobility (p. 14–5, V. 1). When a writer abruptly assumes the role of a minister or an emperor, the shift in their thought process becomes both catastrophic and unstoppable. He was a writer who, among other things, led a well-known party. He drew all his resources from the party and found it impossible to break free, as he centred his life around it. However, he has since become a ruler, a position that places him both outside and above the party; he currently derives his power from all parties, as he considers the interests of each party to be equally important. He now perceives previously unnoticed things and views them from a new perspective. As a result, his entire worldview underwent an immediate transformation. The author firmly believes that the ability to move both vertically and horizontally within society is crucial for the holistic growth of individuals. This unwavering conviction would resemble petrification and cognitive stagnation if all individuals possessed identical notions and remained unchanging in their beliefs.

Next, we turn to his analysis of personal changes in the process of social mobility (p. 35, Vol. 1). The sociologist, using the example of horizontal upward mobility, asserts that the process of social mobility brings about certain personal changes: Every such movement will undoubtedly bring about some degree of change in all aspects of life, including thought, behaviour, and worldview—and this change will be more pronounced the more radical the shift. As a result, the Minister of Education, who was previously the Minister of Police and actively persecuted the press, is always defending it. This enhances Stronin's theory of personal transformations in the process of social mobility and demonstrates how this process also expresses the interconnectedness of the individual, society, and culture.

Stronin also analyzed the individual's egoism as a factor in their personal development (p. 26, Vol. 2). He outlines his theory of personality egoism, which contends that as society becomes more enlightened, its level of selfishness increases. As a result, the solution lies not in the suppression of egoism, but in its comprehension and development. The absence of any activity, particularly egocentric action, explains this.

The sociologist provides the following examples: A person rushes into the water to save a man who is drowning whom he does not know—this, they say, is self-denial; nothing happens—this is the personal interest of the rushing person, the interest of the minute, the unconscious interest, the lofty interest, but still personal, because he considers it his duty at that moment, even though he did not consider it either before or after, without which he would not have acted. Garibaldi dedicates himself entirely to his personal cause, but if he identifies his personal cause with the general one and his own with someone else's, this merely represents a high level of egoism, broad understanding, and his enlightened mood. When he dedicates himself to the people's cause rather than his own personal affairs, nothing happens.

This led to his discussion on the influence of the social environment on the character of the individual (p. 25–6, Vol. 2). Stronin highlights the significance of the social environment's impact on how people develop their personalities, characters, and moral principles. Daily interactions with ordinary people, soldiers, and criminals harden even the mildest dispositions and produce severity, severity, and rudeness of temperament; on the other hand, daily interactions with educated, refined individuals, women, and children cultivate gentleness, meekness, delicacy, and timidity.

In addition, he lists some related professions that fall into the first category, such as officer, landowner, police officer, and district head, and the second category, which includes teacher, professor, doctor, and valet.

Next, he discussed the role of goal-setting in the life of a person (p. 27, Vol. 2): The issue of goal-setting in a person's life holds a specific position in the sociological side of personality research. Understanding the factors that support and hinder goals is necessary for success; one must be able to differentiate between causes and effects.

Finally, he concluded with a conversation on the influence of socioeconomic, legal, and other factors on the development of personal qualities (p. 12, Vol. 3). Stronin asserts that the same individual, at least in part, improves in better circumstances: prosperity leads to greater independence, pride, and self-reliance; acknowledgment of one's rights leads to greater self-assurance and vigour; and so on. It follows that society, through its economic, political, and legal structures, has a significant impact on an individual's growth by meeting, or conversely, her needs and interests.

Therefore, from the sociological perspective of its study, Stronin's personality is a systemic trait due to its participation in social relationships and its capacity to function both as an object and the subject of activity.

Stronin, as a teacher, shared his pedagogical knowledge in the area of personality education within a group. He defended the ideas of the personal approach to education, the importance of self-education, and the collective in becoming a full-fledged citizen. While teaching in gymnasiums, the teacher noticed a low level of development of collective principles in the classrooms of educational institutions. He began to explore the origins of this problem and focused on the mentor's personality as the main organizer of the educational process. Stronin was a vocal opponent of the notion that teachers, engulfed by their authority, often overlooked the primary goal of their activities—the education and upbringing of future citizens who will be responsible for shaping a new era. We examine the two components of Stronin's social-pedagogical personality study:

a) **Disclosure of personality oriented technology in education and the need for their use** (Stronin, 1883, pp. 12–13): According to him, education's goal is to enable the original development of personality through the process of individualization in the educational system. According to a

Russian sociologist, exams and transfers are not necessary: "Let every man put himself in the class, which is enough; otherwise, the school prefers itself to the student and sacrifices reality for ideals" (1883, p. 10). In our opinion, the application of Stronin's ideas to the examination of this issue is highly illogical and ludicrous.

The educational process is a system, and tests and examinations play a key role in regulating student understanding. This verification form facilitates the sharing of teacher-student feedback and enables the estimation of the calibre of instruction and the degree of student training. Therefore, regardless of their level of ability or propensity for one activity over another, all students must go through a process of knowledge verification.

b) **Bringing up the issue of poor educational quality** (1883, p. 32): It calls our attention to the fact that pedagogy is constantly focused on the educational content, such as the degree of subject specificity and the duration of teaching hours. As a result, the use of various pedagogical technologies and the lack of pedagogical materials do not receive adequate attention. According to Stronin, "how to educate and who to teach" is the most important issue. Thus, the humanistic paradigm takes into account the pedagogical aspect of personality research, where the fundamental goal of the pedagogical process is to facilitate the development of a person's skills, personality, spiritual development, morality, and self-realization. From a pedagogical perspective, personality, according to him, is the spiritually and morally evolved individual who is capable of self-improvement.

An analysis of its theoretical and practical aspects revealed some convergence with Stronin's personality structure concept.

Stronin's concept of personality structure centres on the aesthetic component, which shapes the personality into the ideal form of a harmonious human (see Figure 3.1). The five senses—hearing, sight, smell—express external feelings, while internal feelings like love, hatred, and fear are some examples of these ideal-forming concepts.

According to Stronin, the three parameters that make up the theoretical side of the study of personalities are psycho-physiological functions and organic necessities; religious consciousness and behaviour; status and social functions/roles. Thus, the theoretical element suggests the contemplative, intellectual personality's activity, represented through the collaboration of three personality's sides: man as a psycho-physiological creature, religious man, and social man, according to Stronin.

The system of value orientations of the personality, which is composed of three blocks, presents the practical side of personality study: selfish

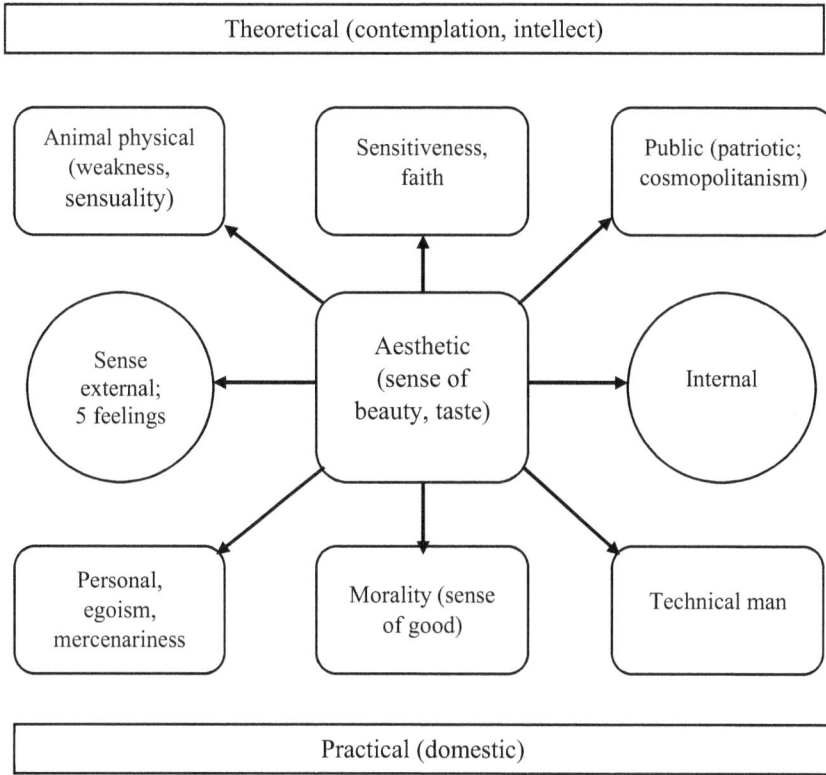

FIGURE 3.1   The structure of personality (Oganyan, 2016).

personality traits; moral qualities and values of goodness and justice; and material and economic values and interests. Thus, Stronin analyzes the practical component in three personality types: the selfish man, the moral man, and the economic man.

Sternin's theory states that a person's personality is made up of their objective and subjective personal qualities, which develop and play out as they participate in various activities and are influenced by their groups and organizations.

Stronin, as a representative of the Russian sociology organic school, places significant emphasis on morality while analyzing the personality in a particular setting. The following points provide an analysis of the ethical component of personality study: (a) the interdependence of fear and moral quality—the lie (p. 10, Vol. 1); (b) the interdependence of external and internal displays of personality qualities (p. 1, Vol. 2); (c) the features of moral qualities and personality's feelings displayed in public relations (p. 21, Vol. 2); (d) the moral qualities characteristic of different social strata (pp. 22–3,

Vol. 2); (e) features displaying the content of types of love (pp. 23–4, Vol. 2; pp. 23–4, Vol. 4).

Conclusion

The development of a methodological framework for the investigation of social phenomena was necessary for the growth of sociological science in the 19th century. Methodology collectively refers to the foundational concepts, approaches, and methods of any science, or the collection of research techniques employed in it. Stronin, a positivist, created a new system of theoretical knowledge based on the gathering, processing, and analysis of social facts. The laws and procedures of the natural sciences form the foundation of this system of knowledge. His mechanical and biological interpretations of social life's events set him apart. People regard his sociological concept as a harmonious, coherent, and logical system of interconnected ideas, which encompasses the nature of social knowledge, its structure and methodology, the specifics of sociology as a science, its object and subject, the nature, structure, and dynamics of society, and the patterns of its functioning and evolution.

Stronin's three important publications, including History and Method, Politics as a Science, and Public History, function as a comprehensive textbook on sociology and cover the entire field. Stronin's works are frequently subject to both positive and negative evaluations based on political ideologies. According to N. K. Mikhailovsky, Stronin examines group conflicts and the struggle of social groups using the Darwinian law of the struggle for existence. He says the strongest "survived" by exploiting the weakest. However, the biological philosophy, which elevated the victor in the social battle, was abhorrent and inaccurate from the perspective of subjective sociology. In general, Mikhailovsky thought that defending the root causes of social inequality amounted to an admission of guilt for this injustice. P. N. Tkachev, who shared Stronin's opinion that his principles were primarily social conservatism, was heavily criticized. E. V. de Roberti, who largely praised "Politics as a Science," asserted that Stronin's work gained more scientific value as he identified more specific generalizations and social norms. According to N. I. Kareev, the monograph "History of the Public" is a sociological attempt to establish a theory of historical progress based on patterns of social occurrences. He praised Stronin's set of sociological notions as one of the best in Russian sociological science.

References

Akmalova, A., Kapitsyn, V. M., Mironov, A. V., and Mokshin, V. K. (2011). *Dictionary-reference Book on Sociology*. Educational Edition.

Brockhaus, F. A., and Efron, I. A. (1890). Stronin Alexander Ivanovich. In Энциклопед ический словарь Брокгауза и Ефрона—Алфавитный каталог—Э лектронная библиотека Руниверс (Encyclopedic Dictionary of Brockhaus and Efron). https://runivers.ru/lib/book3182/

Matyushenko, G., and Samsonova, N. G. (2014). Russian Philosophy. Encyclopedia. 2nd ed., modified and supplemented. Edited by M. A. Olive. Compiled by P. P. Apryshko and A. P. Polyakov. Moscow, 614–615.

Nemeth, T. (2018). Positivism in Late Tsarist Russia: Its Introduction, Penetration, and Diffusion. In J. Feichtinger, F. L. Fillafer, and J. Surman (Eds.), *The Worlds of Positivism: A Global Intellectual History, 1770–1930* (pp. 273–291). Springer International Publishing. https://doi.org/10.1007/978-3-319-65762-2_10

Oganyan, K. "Ideological Intersections of Personality's Analysis In Armenian and Russian Social-Philosophical Thought." *Wisdom*, 1, no. 6 (2016): 87–93). http://dx.doi.org/10.24234/wisdom.v1i6.67.

Parhomenco, G. (2012). А.И. Стронин—Педагог, философ, социолог и публицист XIX века | Летопись Белогорья (A.I. Stronin—Teacher, philosopher, sociologist and publicist of the 19th century). https://belstory.ru/goroda/rakitnoe/a-i-stronin-pedagog-filosof-sotsiolog-i-publitsist-xix-veka.html

Stronin, A. I. (1861). Azbuka po metode V. Zolotova dlia iuzhno-russkogo kraia [ABC: Zolotov's method for the South-Russian region]. Poltava: Gubernskaia tipografiia (Poltava Provincial Printing House).

Stronin, A. I. (1869). History and Method. A. M. Kotomin. https://viewer.rusneb.ru/ru/000199_000009_003582757?page=3&rotate=0&theme=white

Stronin, A. I. (1872). Politics as a science (Политика как наука—Стронин Александр Иванович). F. S. Sushchinsky. https://rusneb.ru/catalog/000199_000009_003602684/

Stronin, A. I. (1883). Teoriya lichnosti (Personality's theory). Otdel rukopisei Rossiiskoi nacional'noi biblioteki g.Sankt-Peterburg. F. 752, D. 13, L. 10. No 28.

Stronin, A. I. (1885). Public History (История общественности—Стронин Александр Иванович). M-va put. message (A. Benke). https://rusneb.ru/catalog/000199_000009_003649344/

Stronin, A. I. (2013). Teoriya lichnosti (A personality's theory) (po materialam rukopisi). Avt.-sost. Nauchnogo issledovaniya K.K.Oganyan. 2-e izd., dop. I pererab. Moskva. INFRA-M (Seriya: Nauchnayamysl').

Valerievna, S. E. (2006). Социологическая концепция А. И. Стронина (Sociological concept of A. I. Stronin). http://www.dslib.net/teoria-sociologii/sociologicheskaja-koncepcija-a-i-stronina.html

4

PAVEL LILIENFELD

Common patterns between the nature and society

Liudmila Zhdanovich

Pavel Feodorovich Lilienfeld-Toal (1829–1903) lived in an era when sociology as a science was at the very beginning of its formation. Lilienfeld's interest in the structure of society and the mechanisms of its functioning was directly related to the fact that in the second half of the 19th century, the issues of social development in Russia were particularly acute. During this period, enormous social changes took place in Russia. Serfdom was abolished, and the process of much-needed liberal reforms designed to modernize Russian society began. Lilienfeld was at the very centre of this process. He was one of those who carried out the peasant reform of 1861 as a conciliator and laid the foundations for the activities of local self-government as chairman of the zemstvo council. An indefatigable worker, he had always known how to find room for scientific research alongside the duties of administration (Worms 1903: 265). As governor, he had to observe fluctuations in government policy caused by the radicalization of the social movement; as a member of the Senate, he witnessed the strengthening of conservative tendencies in the domestic politics of the Russian Empire. Throughout his long and eventful life, he successfully combined the career of an influential government official and public figure with a scientific rethinking of Russian and world reality (Zhdanovich 2017: 81–2).

Having received an excellent education at one of the most prestigious educational institutions in Russia, Lilienfeld continued self-education throughout his life. He spoke several foreign languages and was familiar with the leading biological and medical theories of his time. Lilienfeld's ideas developed within the framework of positivist philosophy under the strong influence of Auguste Comte. The formation of the views of one of the first

DOI: 10.4324/9781003541004-5

Russian sociologists was influenced by a number of prominent thinkers and scientists, including Rene Descartes, Francis Bacon, Charles Darwin, Rudolf Virchow, and Ernst Haeckel.

It is often spoken of the need to move from theory to practice. Lilienfeld did the opposite. He built his theoretical arguments on the basis of his richest practical experience. He published his first work, Fundamental Principles of Political Economy, in 1860, a year before the abolition of serfdom in Russia. In 1868, before taking the post of Courland governor, he published the work "Land and Freedom," in which he outlined his views on the "peasant question" that developed in Russia in the second half of the 1860s, analyzing the state of the peasant economy as well as the difficulties faced by the peasantry after the abolition of serfdom. This book was the result of Lilienfeld's reflections on the knowledge he received after several years of work in the countryside as a conciliator and chairman of the zemstvo council (P.L. 1868: 32–33).

Lilienfeld devoted the next quarter of a century to the development of an organic concept of society, the foundations of which he outlined in his 1872 work Thoughts on the Social Science of the Future. In an expanded and supplemented form, this work was published in German a few years later. In the preface to the edition, he noted the following:

> Every day the unfruitfulness of the scholastico-dogmatical method of treating political and social questions, which still prevails not only in science but in the daily press, becomes more evident and more striking. In the realm of natural science, the untenability of this method has been recognized for centuries. Conviction of the equal untenability and harmfulness of this method in the realm of social science has prompted the author to devote himself to this work.
>
> *(P. L. 1873: V)*

Lilienfeld wrote his subsequent works in German or French and published them abroad. This was due to the fact that the formation of sociology in the Russian Empire took place in extremely difficult conditions. The ruling circles were wary of the new science, since the first Russian sociologists were active in politics, raising significant social issues and giving assessments of the most important political events. Lilienfeld was one of those thinkers who suffered from this policy of the Tsarist government. He published his work, Thoughts on the Social Science of the Future, under the initials P. L. The censorship authorities suspected that the author of the work could be Pyotr Lavrov, known for his socialist views. A government order was issued to withdraw the book from the bookshops and public libraries. As a result, Lilienfeld, as governor of Courland, had to order the removal of his own book from public access (Kareev 1996: 92).

The Tsarist government was also concerned about the close ties that existed between European and Russian sociologists. Pavel Lilienfeld was one of the few Russian sociological writers whose work was well known outside the Russian Empire. He published in the International Sociological Review, founded in 1892, and also participated in the activities of the International Institute of Sociology, of which he was vice-president and president in 1896 and 1897, respectively (Worms 1903: 265–6).

In his views, Lilienfeld was close to organicism—a direction in sociology whose representatives were Herbert Spencer, Albert Schieffle, Alexander Stronin and others (Small 1924: 1770. In describing the history of the formation of Russian sociology, the historian and sociologist N. I. Kareev attributed the philosophical constructions of P. F. Lilienfeld to "sociological naturalism," at the same time noting that he was in many respects far from Russian sociological literature, completely ignoring it (Kareev 1996: 92). Nevertheless, Lilienfeld's version of the social organism theory is a significant contribution to the development of sociology as a science in Russia. His sociological works became one of the prominent factors in the early stages of the Russian sociological movement.

The subject of sociology

"To what field of human knowledge does sociology belong?"
(Lilienfeld-Toal 2012: 14)

According to Lilienfeld, all sciences can be divided into two groups: speculative and real. In the speculative sciences, such as mathematics, logic, psychology, and metaphysics, man has made his own "I" the main subject of study. Lilienfeld stressed that the subject of study of the real sciences or natural sciences, that is, chemistry, physics, astronomy, and geology, is the surrounding nature. At the beginning of his main work, Thoughts on the Social Science of the Future, Lilienfeld discussed to which field of human knowledge sociology belonged. He acknowledged that the sociologists of that time were faced with a choice—to seek answers to social questions in the depths of their own minds or to turn to the study of what happened outside of man, just as it was done in nature (Lilienfeld-Toal 2012: 14).

According to Lilienfeld, the answer to this question largely depends on the position from which to consider human society. He believed that society was part of a single natural organism and required study from natural science perspectives. In support of his point of view, he tried to define and formulate features that made it possible to attribute sociology to independent positive sciences, that is, sciences that did not operate with abstract concepts but studied real relationships and connections. It should be noted that he did not deny the need for theoretical inferences both in the study of society and nature, but believed that they were not capable of replacing natural scientific methods (Lilienfeld-Toal 2012: 52).

For Lilienfeld, the definition of the subject of sociology as a science was a matter of particular importance because the answer to it depended on the methodology that the new science could use. Lilienfeld based his understanding of the essence and subject of sociology on the principles of positivist philosophy. In his opinion, sociological knowledge could become "positive," that is, capable of positively and successfully solving the problems of society, only when it was based on facts obtained exclusively through experience or observation, that is, by the methods of the natural sciences.

Lilienfeld's works were primarily based on the analogical method. He believed that it was possible to successfully investigate the nature of animals, and of human beings simultaneously by assuming that all these phenomena were regulated by the same laws of behaviour and of evolution. In his opinion, if human society was part of nature, then social science had to become part of natural science and use the method of induction, starting from the facts of nature and going to their causes, a method that discovers general laws from particular cases, ascending from the particular to the general. That is, according to Lilienfeld, induction is the only method that sociology can use if it wants to become a positive science. Induction is the only method by which one can identify the similarities and differences between nature and society and draw an analogy between the action of social forces, that is, the factors that determine the social development of society, and the forces of nature (Lilienfeld-Toal 2012: 61).

Analyzing human society as the main subject of sociology, Lilienfeld noted that the focus of social science should not be human nature, nor its spiritual or physical qualities, but social phenomena; that is, the manifestation of the physical and spiritual forces of a person in the social environment (Lilienfeld-Toal 2012: 30–31). The study of the human spirit, taken by itself, had to remain outside the limits of the social sciences. Lilienfeld opposed any claim that society is unknowable. He believed that the complexity of studying society was due to the fact that it became the subject of science later than nature, and it was much more complex and diverse compared to natural phenomena, which made it difficult to bring it under the influence of constant immutable laws.

At the end of his discussions on the subject of sociology, Lilienfeld comes to the final conclusion: the comparison of human society with nature is a complete analogy. Social science is a continuation of natural science because human society is a continuation of nature (Lilienfeld-Toal 2012: 38).

Society as an organism

Like natural organisms, human society is a real being, it is nothing more than a continuation of nature, it is only a higher expression of the same forces which are at the basis of all natural phenomena. This is the assignment, this is the thesis, which the author has set himself to accomplish and to prove.

(Lilienfeld-Toal 2012)

In the introduction to his first major work, The Fundamental Principles of Political Economy, published in 1860, Lilienfeld wrote: "Human society is not a matter of chance, violence, or human wisdom; it was not started by mutual, open, or silent agreement of its members" (Lileev 1860: 1). Society, according to him, is not an ideal category, as Rousseau, Kant, Fichte, Hegel, and other philosophers have argued for a long time. He believed that society is a certain ratio of people among themselves, and that social organs and the whole society are formed from individual human personalities, just as plant organisms are made up of fibers (Lilienfeld-Toal 2012: 35, 53).

The cellular theory of Rudolf Virchow had a great influence on the formation of Pavel Lilienfeld's views on society. He believed that a social organism is "a multicellular organic being that grows as a result of the reproduction of individuals within the organism and releases them in the event of overgrowth beyond certain limits" (Lilienfeld-Toal 2012: 161).

According to Lilienfeld, human society is composed of cells like the individual organisms of nature. The social cells are the human individuals forming first the family, then the clan, the tribe, the nation and who, coming together by degrees in ever larger groups, end up conglomerating into more or less independent groups. He was sure that, in a more or less distant future, all of humanity would have to form a great organic whole whose parts would be united, in a more or less narrow way, to a central force which would represent, in some form, the trends and ideas of humanity as a unit (Lilienfeld 1896: XXII).

As mentioned before, Lilienfeld considered society an organism in the sense of a natural-real phenomenon, but at the same time believed that in order to recognize the property of reality for human society, there is no need to look for any special organs or feelings in it that would correspond to one or another organ or feeling in a plant, animal, or person. That is, the identity of society and the natural organism does not mean the obligatory presence of external similarity (Lilienfeld-Toal 2012: 93, 96).

He stated that in order to prove the identity of society and the natural organism, it is sufficient to have "a real analogy between the essential properties of society and all bodies of nature in general." According to Lilienfeld, the real analogy lay in "the homology between the economic, juridical, and political aspects of human society, on the one hand, and the physiological, morphological, and individual aspects of organic life, on the other hand." In turn, these sides corresponded to the mechano-chemical, formal, and inorganic-individual sides of inorganic nature (Lilienfeld-Toal 2012: 125–6).

Thus, according to the Russian sociologist, society as a social organism had three main functions: physiological or economic; morphological or legal; and individual (unifying) or political. The economic sphere was analogous to the blood circulation of a biological organism; the law played the same role that is assigned to the nervous system in a biological organism; that is, it controlled the formation of organs and tissues; governments, in turn, corresponded to the central nervous system. According to Lilienfeld, society is an organism because it contains all the distinctive features of an organism: unity, expediency, specialisation of organs, capitalization of forces, and uniqueness of movements. That is, the essential difference between the action of organic forces and inorganic ones was a more expedient movement of nature. It was caused by the improvement of organic life through both internal and external specialisation and the capitalization of forces (Lilienfeld-Toal 2012: 72–3).

Pavel Lilienfeld saw in society a living system that develops and functions, obeying the action of a universal law, which a person is not able to change (Lileev 1860: 5–6). He emphasized that society has integrity and unity. All its organs are interconnected, but at the same time, they specialise in the implementation of specific functions. As a representative of social evolutionizm, Lilienfeld put forward the idea of the gradual development of society. He saw this process as part of the evolution of the Cosmos, the Earth, and the animal world.

A large role in the sociologist's philosophical reasoning is assigned to such concepts as energy, substance, and force. Energy, manifesting itself in the desire for concentration, is transformed into substance. When energy strives for differentiation, it corresponds to force. He stressed that matter without force and force without matter are just as unthinkable as affirmation without negation. Similarly, in the social field, property, law, and power are nothing more than freedom concentrated in specific forms, properties, and positions. At the same time, freedom is nothing more than property, law, and power acting outward (Lilienfeld-Toal 2012: 72–3).

Continuing this thought, Lilienfeld noted that a person can manifest his spiritual and physical powers only with the help of a substance. When human labour interacts with a natural force, it becomes matter. For Lilienfeld, labour was the combination of the physiological forces of natural organisms with the forces of human bodies; the combination of matter and force (Lilienfeld-Toal 2012: 57–8).

The natural diversity of the world, according to Lilienfeld, is caused by the different orientations of energy, which he correlates with such concepts as causality and expediency. In the process of the development of organic phenomena, the ratio of causality and expediency gradually changes. There is a constant process of differentiation and integration of energy. He wrote,

In nature and in human society, the higher and more varied develop from the simpler and lower; social motives, irritations in the animal and plant environment, chemical, physical, and mechanical forces are only different expressions of one and the same: energy that is differentiated and integrated at the same time.

(Lilienfeld-Toal 2012: 56–7)

In his work "Thoughts on the Social Science of the Future," he noted: "To invent for human society any other principle of causality and expediency than that which permeates all of nature means to deny or not be aware of that inextricable connection that unites everything into one whole" (Lilienfeld-Toal 2012: 46).

In emphasizing the similarity between natural and social organisms, Lilienfeld noted that the lymphatic, circulatory, and muscular systems, as well as the skeletal system, are absent in the social organism. As a consequence, the social organism consists primarily of the nervous system, which is made up of people. However, people are not only the nerve cells of society but also the intercellular substance created by them, which is formed from everything that people have developed (houses, railways, books, works of art, money, laws, etc.). In developing the physiology and morphology of the social organism, Lilienfeld gave primacy to the major factor of every human association, starting with the family and going up to the state and the whole human race. To him, it is the nervous system, the source of all social action. He also argued that the intercellular substance of individual organisms corresponds in the social organism to wealth produced, exchanged, and consumed. Any action of the social nervous system is similar to the physiological action of individual organisms endowed with nervous systems. He also insisted that the social organism's specific nerve energies are the same as in natural organisms, not just metaphorically but literally (Lilienfeld 1896: 8–11).

Lilienfeld admitted that the primary distinction between a social and a biological organism is that society is less integrated than an organism. He pointed out that organic nature itself presents three degrees of development. The first is that plants cannot move autonomously, either together as a whole or separately as parts. The second is that animals can move freely but only as individuals, that is, as parts. Third, a social aggregate can move freely both as a whole and in its parts. Thus, it is only in human society that nature realises in all its fullness the highest degree of organic life: the autonomy of the same individual organism in the parts and in the whole. This difference means only that the social organism is the highest class of organism, and nothing more (Lilienfeld 1896: 307). He believed that the individual and the social system were not in an incurable conflict but enjoyed a space of autonomy and movement that mutually enhanced them.

Turning to the problem of the relationship between an individual and society, Lilienfeld argued that a separate individual should not be the subject of sociology. The study of people as individual members of society should be dealt with by philosophy. The task of social science was to study the properties and strengths of individuals only in the context of society (Lilienfeld-Toal 2012: 37).

As a representative of organicism, Lilienfeld understood society as an organism and the individual as its cell. That is, a person, according to the thinker, was the simplest cellular element of a social organism. The interaction of individuals in a social organism is identical to the life processes taking place in the human body; that is, it is similar to the interaction of cells in the nervous system and especially in its higher organs, which are material carriers of individual feelings, thoughts, and desires.

Lilienfeld turned to the teachings of Charles Darwin to analyse the role and place of man in society. He saw the difference between higher vertebrates and man solely in the degree of development, noting that man owes his development to social life. Unlike animals, man, according to the sociologist, is a social being and

> just as the organisms of nature are the result of the differentiation and integration of forces under the influence of the surrounding physical environment, in the same way the higher nervous organs of man are the result of the differentiation and integration of the same forces under the influence of society.
>
> *(Lilienfeld-Toal 2012: 216–7)*

He did not believe that the difference between man and animals was enormous. Lilienfeld's significance of a person comes down to the fact that a person is a part of society, and his physical and spiritual properties determine the economic, legal, and political structure of society; the features of the development of various social groups; as well as social and state organisms. The same thing happens in the natural organism, where individual plant and animal fibres determine the composition of the whole organism.

At the same time, Lilienfeld stressed the importance of society in forming the individual as a member of society. He wrote:

> If man, from the physical point of view, is first of all a product of nature, he is, from the point of view of intelligence, above all a product of society. The most important organs of the nervous system form, develop, differentiate, and integrate in response to the social milieu, just as the purely physical part of man forms and develops in response to the physical milieu through natural differentiation and integration of forces. The

economic activity of society, work, customs, habits, laws, political liberty, authority, religion, science, art, in short, all of social life, forms and educates man, gives to his efforts, to his intellectual, moral and aesthetic needs, this or that direction, pushing in this or that sense the complete development of the superior organs of the nervous system.

(Lilienfeld-Toal 2012: 261)

Social progress and its criteria

Lilienfeld paid much attention to the problem of social dynamics. Associating progress with the complication of forms of development, he believed that any form of life is a gradual improvement. He attributed the concept of progress to both inanimate and living nature. According to Lilienfeld, progress in the form of an expedient and consistent interaction of matter and force was an integral part of social life. He derives the laws of progress for all three areas of society: political progress, which was manifested in the strengthening of power and the expansion of political freedom; economic progress, which consisted of increasing property and expanding economic freedom; and legal progress, which included the strengthening of law and the development of legal freedom. In turn, he believed that regression was a disorder, a weakening of the principles of power, law, property, and restriction of freedom (Lilienfeld-Toal 2012: 91).

Thus, Lilienfeld saw freedom as the primary criterion for social progress, which he defined as societal freedom rather than individual freedom. In particular, he noted that "one of the essential symptoms of progress is not only the strengthening of power but concurrently an enlargement of freedom". At the same time, he spoke about a certain level of freedom only, not absolute freedom. He stated that when power becomes despotism and freedom is suppressed, various elements of the social organism's hierarchical structure become unstable, collide, and lead to the disorganisation of social life, which inevitably leads to the emergence of pathological conditions (Lilienfeld 1896: 164).

However, freedom in society can only be relative. Lilienfeld argued that unconditional freedom is impossible in society, just as unlimited movement is impossible in nature. In order to determine the measure of freedom that is permissible, it is necessary to determine the average economic, legal, and political energy developed by the members of a given society at a given historical moment.

Lilienfeld also attributed the diversity of goals and the predominance of the spiritual factor, that is, expediency over causality and necessity, to the criteria for social progress.

"The higher a society stands in comparison with other societies," he wrote, "the more expedient and reasonable its development, the more the struggle that determines its development is carried out with less effort, the more reasonable the goals to which society strives."

(Lilienfeld-Toal 2012: 86)

Social pathology

Lilienfeld was among the first sociological writers who developed the concept of social pathology. He believed that one of the tasks of sociology is to identify the essence and causes of social diseases, anomalies, and various deviations that exist in society due to the fact that it is a real organism. Sociology must also find a means of correcting them. In his work, Social Pathology, the author distinguished between anomalies and pathologies in the development of social organisms. Social disease, unlike an anomaly, takes place in the process of the life of society, while an anomaly is a phenomenon that is alien to the life process. In studying the issue, Lilienfeld drew on factual material from a number of sciences, including physiology, anthropology, and medicine.

The starting point for the formation of his views on the problem of social pathology was Rudolf Virchow's theory of cellular pathology. He considered it to be one of the most striking conquests of modern science. Studying the question of the causes of social pathologies, Lilienfeld noted the following: "The common source of any normal or abnormal activity in the human body arises from the degeneracy or abnormal action of the single cell, as the elementary anatomical unit of which every organism is constructed" (Lilienfeld 1896: 20–1).

Lilienfeld distinguished between a normal and diseased organism and then, by analogy, between a normal and diseased society. He agreed with Virchow that there was no essential and absolute difference between the normal state and the pathological state of an organism. He stated that society attacked by disease does not present a state essentially different from that of a normal society. At the same time, he stressed that as every pathological disease derives from a pathological state of the cell, likewise every social disease has its cause in a degeneration or abnormal action of the individual who constitutes the elementary anatomical unit of the social organism. The pathological state manifests itself in an individual's or a group's activities that are untimely, out of place, or indicate overexcitement or a lack of energy. According to Lilienfeld, deviation from the normal state meant an action outside of the necessary time, outside of the necessary place, or outside the limits of excitation prescribed by the normal state. The pathological state of an organism therefore implies either an aberration in relation to time, or an aberration in relation to place, or an aberration in relation to the energy of action of the single cell. Thus, a heterology is, wrote Lilienfeld, always either a heterochrony, or a heterotopia, or finally a heterometry (Lilienfeld 1896: 24).

Lilienfeld also raised the problem of the ageing of the social organism, as a result of which it turns into an inorganic mechanism. He stated that as long as the cell does not exceed certain aberration limits, it can be reduced to its normal state; it can heal; however, once the extreme limits are reached, the cell degenerates and becomes disorganized; it dies. At the same time, the death of a single cell or even of an association of cells does not necessarily imply the disorganisation or the death of the whole body. Degenerated or dead cells can be replaced by other new ones. This process of regeneration and accumulation of new energies is shared by all organisms and is the fundamental principle of organic life's progressive evolution (Lilienfeld 1896: 20–1).

Lilienfeld was also aware of the germ theory of disease. He agreed with the idea that each disease corresponds to a specific bacillus. He identified certain social diseases as similarly caused by "specific parasites." Pavel Lilienfeld distinguished three types of "parasitism" common in society, stressing that while the individual organism is haunted by specific bacilli for each disease, the social organism is infested by economic, legal, and political parasites. These three categories of parasites are subdivided into several classes and species, each of which corresponds to a special disease for the social organism (Lilienfeld 1896: 46–7). He stated that all exploitation under the aegis of legality implies a case of legal parasitism; any abuse of power, a case of political parasitism. There are also agricultural parasites that exploit for the purpose of immediate enrichment of landed property by depleting the soil, destroying forests, deteriorating buildings and inventory, and making real estate a speculative asset.

Illustrating his views on social parasitism, Lilienfeld turned to examples from the Russian Empire. He wrote that a large part of the land in Russia is exploited by a whole newly formed class of entrepreneurs who have the characteristic traits of agricultural pests. An industrial parasite is a manufacturer who competes with the producers of his specialty by delivering products of questionable quality, little solidity, and adulteration. Commercial pests are those who stand between the producer and the consumer with the intention of exploiting them without reducing the exchange of products. However, according to Lilienfeld, the most dangerous bacilli of the economic sphere are represented by those who engage in usury in any form. He described them as leeches that feed on the blood of the people (Lilienfeld 1896: 46–7).

As for political parasitism, Lilienfeld believed that it is represented by all those who, by their abilities and their morality, do not meet the requirements of their political and official position; by all the political agitators who have in view only their ambition or personal interest. He argued that the government that creates sinecures or charges the budget for the upkeep of an excessive number of employees only breeds parasites (Lilienfeld 1896: 48).

At the same time, Lilienfeld pointed out that social parasitism has a different degree of danger to society. The most dangerous parasites are those that violate the fundamental principles that determine society's organic life: laws that protect citizens' personal safety and property. The government, as the central organ of the nervous system, has to neutralise the negative impact of parasitism by initiating the process of reforms (Lilienfeld 1896: 48).

It was already mentioned that, according to Lilienfeld, the social organism consists of two anatomical elements: the nervous system and the intercellular substance. He believed that this was the reason why society as a social organism suffers mostly from diseases of the social nervous system. Lilienfeld found in the social organism analogues of such diseases of the nervous system as hysteria, paralysis, monomania, asthenia, and amnesia (Lilienfeld 1896: 59, 88). He wrote the following:

> It is only in the figurative sense that we have designated until today the state of a country in the grip of an economic, legal, or political crisis, such as a state of insanity, delirium, or paralysis. After observing the existence of a social nervous system, it is no longer necessary to think of these states figuratively, but in a completely real sense.
>
> *(Lilienfeld 1896: 55–6)*

Discussing the problem, Lilienfeld mentioned that psychiatry encompasses all abnormalities of an individual's nervous system. Madness may take the form of hysteria, asthenia, paralysis, monomania, amnesia, and others, each of which each is further subdivided into different categories. However, he argued that hysteria is never the result of degeneration of the nervous system as a whole. It is the result of the disorderly and violent actions of a small group of cells. In the same way, most crises and revolutions were caused by a small group of ambitious or fanatical individuals. It is through speech, writing, and the press that they have led the masses to violent actions, sometimes salutary if it was a question of fighting a more dangerous evil, but for the most part destructive and pernicious (Lilienfeld 1896: 55–6, 60).

Considering the social anomalies of the intercellular substance, Pavel Lilienfeld noted that they affect all spheres of society, but he paid special attention to the economic side of it. According to the Russian thinker, the intercellular substance of organisms is analogous in the social organism to money and financial exchange. He believed that one of the major deviations in the economic sphere is the concentration of property in the hands of a minority. This does not imply that he advocated for universal equality, but he was convinced that only distribution based on free competition could benefit society's development and promote progress. The diversity of forms of ownership is another condition for the absence of serious economic and political problems in the state. Lilienfeld noted that the presence of different forms of ownership allows the state to develop immunity to various economic diseases (Lilienfeld 1896: 97–8, 111).

Lilienfeld distinguished several types of social organisms that evolved over time and differed in their morphological structure and the structure of their central organs. He argued that any drastic change in the political, economic, or legal spheres of the formed type of society can be dangerous since it can lead to a weakening of the social nervous system. Pavel Lilienfeld also argued that social inequality is a natural phenomenon. It was established by the nature of social hierarchy and social relations, which arose under the influence of laws that determine the development of organic life as a whole. As a result, wealth in society is distributed and concentrated in the hands of individual members in accordance with the natural laws that exist in society (Lilienfeld 1896: 94, 151).

Lilienfeld believed that the normal process of the life of society, in contrast to the pathological one, is a harmonious relationship of all functions (economic, legal, and political). Any living being strives for harmony, but the laws of living nature can only be realised through the struggle of various elements that form part of any organic body. In this regard, Lilienfeld believed that the class struggle that exists in society is a necessary condition for its stability and harmony; the role of the state as a social institution is to restore the balance lost by society. The state, with the help of legislation, must regulate the physical and spiritual state of the social organism and timely resolve the contradictions that arise in the course of the natural struggle of individuals.

Some researchers have characterised Lilienfeld as a supporter of social Darwinism. Despite the fact that the sociologist acknowledged that a struggle for existence existed in society, he believed that the process was distinct from what occurred between organisms in nature. He wrote the following:

> Every cell and every group of cells never cease to struggle for existence within any organism of nature. In the same way, every individual and every association of individuals are destined by their nature to struggle against the opposing interests of their fellows. But this struggle has a productive and regenerative character only insofar as it does not end in extinction and exhaustion of power and conflicting interests. As this struggle reaches higher spheres, as the psychic factor gains ground on the physical factor in the march of social evolution, the struggle loses its exterminating and inhuman character and allows itself to be influenced more and more by altruistic principles and by the common interest.
>
> *(Lilienfeld 1896: 46)*

To summarise, Pavel Fedorovich Lilienfeld-Toal was unquestionably a vivid example of an extraordinary thinker. He attempted to avoid the extremes of idealism and materialism in his theoretical constructions, condemning dogmatism as the root cause of social intolerance and fanaticism. His understanding of human society, as well as sociology as a science, its role, and methods, all contributed to the establishment of sociology. He also contributed to the translation of concepts and principles developed in biology and medicine into broader social thinking.

Lilienfeld remained true to the end to the ideas and principles formulated in his main works. In the introduction to his work, Thoughts on the Social Science of the Future, he wrote the following:

If this work does not prove as useful as is hoped, if it does not help to extend the scope of social science and to give it firmer foundations, the reason must be in the inadequacy of the powers of the author and of the means at his disposal, not in fault of the method nor in the untenability of the principles upon which it rests, and upon which alone, in the author's deepest conviction, the entire structure of the social sciences can be durably erected.

(Lilienfeld-Toal 2012: 2)

References

Kareev, N.I. 1996. *Osnovy russkoy sotsiologii [The Foundation of Russian sociology]*. Saint-Petersburg: Ivan Lymbah.

Lileev, P. 1860. *Osnovnie nachala politicheskoi economii [Fundamental Principles of Political Economy]*. Saint-Petersburg.

Lilienfeld, Paul de. 1896. *La pathologie sociale. [Social Pathology.] Avec une préface de René Worms. Bibliothèque Sociologique Internationale, II*. Paris: V. Giard et E. Brière.

Lilienfeld-Toal, Pavel Feodorovich. 2012. *Mysli o sotsial'noi naukie budushchego [Thoughts on the Social Science of the Future]*. Moscow: Librokom.

P.L. 1868. *Zemlia i volia [Land and Liberty]*. Saint-Petersburg: V. Bezobrazov and Co.

P.L. 1873. *Gedanken über die Socialwissenschaft der Zukunft [Thoughts on the Social Science of the Future]*. Mitau: E. Behre. Vol. 1.

Small, A.W. 1924. Some Contributions to the History of Sociology. Section XVII. The Attempt (1860–80) to Reconstruct Economic Theory on a Sociological Basis. *American Journal of Sociology*, Vol. 30, No. 2 (September), pp. 177–194.

Worms, R. 1903. Paul de Lilienfeld. *Revue Internationale de Sociologie*, Vol. 11e Année, No. 4 (April), pp. 265–267.

Zhdanovich, L.N. 2017. P.F. Lilienfeld-Toal o zemle i vole v poreformennoy rossii [P.F. Lilienfeld-Toal on land and freedom in post-reform Russia]. In Nikulin, V.N. (ed.): *North-West in the Agrarian History of Russia*. Kaliningrad: Immanuel Kant Baltic Federal University, pp. 81–88.

5

NIKOLAY KONSTANTINOVICH MIKHAYLOVSKY

The Narodnik movement—background and critique

Alex Moore

The Narodnik movement is often regarded as a defining shift within Russian political thought. While often regarded as the first populist movement, many ideological aspects of the Narodnik movement would later be carried over within the Russian Revolution. One such notable figure among the Narodnik movement was Nikolay Konstantinovich Mikhaylovsky. This chapter will begin with a brief overview of the Narodnik movement, their aim, tactics, and ideology, and its relationship to the academic literature surrounding populist studies. It will analyze the theories of the leading figure of the Narodniks, Nikolay Konstantinovich Mikhaylovsky. To conclude, it will access the lasting impacts of the Narodniks and Mikhaylovsky among the larger scope of Russian social political thought.

In 1861, Tsar Alexander II of Russia enacted the emancipation of the serfs, widely seen as one of the major liberal reforms within tsarist Russia, thus abolishing serfdom within Russia. The emancipation allowed peasants to own property, marry without their owners' consent, purchase land from landlords, and own businesses. Yet, it should be noted that household serfs only gained freedom and not the right to own land. This is largely due to the fact that prior to the emancipation, peasants were divided into two categories: those who lived on state-owned land and those who lived on private land. Only those on private land were considered serfs.

While previous efforts to abolish serfdom had largely been unsuccessful, with a few notable regional exceptions, such as Congress Poland under Napoleon Bonaparte in 1807, and Estonia in 1816, tsarist Russia was one of the few notable remaining European countries that had not abolished serfdom. This, along with Russia's loss in the Crimean war of 1853–1856, made

DOI: 10.4324/9781003541004-6

the government aware of its political and economic shortcomings. Thus, this solidified within the state's mindset that serfdom needed to be abolished. Initially, the landlords were against granting the serfs the ability to own land as they feared it would lead to their loss of economic supremacy. This, along with the revolutions of 1848 in western Europe, made the nobility wary of creating a proletariat class. However, as a result of a third of serfs being mortgaged to the state or to banks, there was no other alternative but to accept full emancipation.

Yet, emancipation only resulted in emancipation in theory as opposed to in practice. One aspect of this was the result of newly formed localized governments, resulting in landowners gaining a stronger political voice. Also, many of the freed serfs were unable to afford adequate amounts of land to survive. Likewise, in order to pay taxes, many of the former serfs had to sell the majority of their crops. This also forced many of the freed serfs to rent land from wealthy landlords, and essentially resulted in a similar social structure to that which was previously experienced under serfdom. This created civil unrest and resentment among the now freed serfs, with many peasants being neglectful of their fields, resulting in famine in many portions of Russia.

This resulted in several uprisings with a harsh response from the government and landlords. Those responsible for the uprisings were oftentimes severely punished, while the landlords received almost no reprimanding for their actions. This led to increased support for laissez-faire capitalism among the peasantry, which was taking place in Western Europe at the time.

Another consequence was the rise of various social movements in support of political reforms. One such movement to emerge was the Narodnik movement. The Narodnik movement is widely regarded as being the first populist movement, as "Narodnik" is Russian for "Populace." It is also widely regarded as being the first populist party due to its founding in 1861, whereas the People's Party, or Populist Party, in the USA, did not emerge until 1891. The Narodnik movement, Narodniki, advocated for the overthrow of the tsarist regime through the use of propaganda among the peasantry as a means of liberating them from what the Narodniki saw as the slavery of the peasantry.

Yet unlike most populist movements, the Narodniki did not arise from the peasantry, but rather arose from Russian intellectuals. The Narodniki believed that by supporting and strengthening the then existing peasant communes, and through the use of propaganda, they could educate the peasantry to revolt against the tsar. The movement was strongly influenced by Karl Marx; yet unlike Marx, they did not believe that industrial capitalism was necessary to achieve socialism. Rather, the Narodniki believed that industrial capitalism could be forgone and thus move directly from feudalism to socialism. Thus, not only were the Narodniki modifying Marx on socialism coming about through industrialization but were modifying Marx's view of history that socialism could come about in other countries, such as Russia, which was largely agrarian at the time.

While the Narodniki believed the peasantry to be the agrarian equivalent of the Marxian workers and the landowners to be that of the bourgeoisie, there was another noticeable difference between Narodniki thought and Marxist thought. This was the idea of the so-called "Great Man theory," or the idea that history is shaped by exceptional individuals who use their alleged superior abilities to shape the course of history. This was because the movement saw the peasantry as being too passive and submissive, and thus in need of a leader to not only stir up a revolution but to guide them along the way. Yet, many Narodniks favoured an immediate revolution that went beyond intellectual dialogue and thought.

Yet, it should be noted that this did not necessarily carry out according to plan as the Narodniki had initially hoped. One reason being that while the Narodniki spent an immense amount of time studying the peasantry and their way of life, and even went as far as dressing in a similar fashion to the peasants, to help increase revolutionary sentiment, the peasantry met the movement with suspicion. This was largely due to the Narodniki not being accepted as peasants but rather being viewed as being outsiders. This was largely due largely by the movement's support for agrarian socialism as opposed to the peasantry's support for industrialized capitalism. Furthermore, while the Narodnik movement's offshoot, Narodnaya Volya ("People's Will"), was eventually successful in staging a revolution against the tsar (which was escalated by increased regime persecution against the movement) and ultimately resulted in the tsar's death, this further distanced the peasantry as their response to this movement was largely seen as too radical a motion for the peasantry to support. Many of the rural peasants were loyal to the tsar and the Russian Orthodox Church, for which the movement placed large amounts of blame on the peasants' societal ills.

To further elaborate on this disconnect, the Narodniki erroneously perceived the peasants to be poorly dressed people and thus intended to imitate this image as a means to gain their trust. Yet, in actuality, the peasants saw this as outsiders poorly imitating their way of life, with little to no authority of their own, as opposed to the authority of the tsar and the Orthodox Church, which was held in high esteem by the peasantry.

This would result in a tarnished view of the peasantry from the Narodniki and further widen the gap between the two. This was only widened by the peasants being largely illiterate and thus unable to read pamphlets distributed by the movement. A final issue of disconnect was the idea of equality of the sexes, which was advocated by the Narodniki, as well as many other socialist movements, as opposed to a more traditional way of life that was practiced by the peasants. All in all, the Narodnik movement failed to realize that the average peasant was more concerned with access to basic life necessities and thus had little time to engage in intellectual discussions regarding socialism and revolution.

Analysis and critique

The first issue that arises is whether the Narodnik movement can be truly labelled a populist movement. The term populism, and its definition, is highly contested within academia. Much like most theoretical conceptualizations, defining populism is arguably a daunting task. While there is much debate over the nature of populism, the most widely cited definition is that of the Dutch political scientist, Cas Mudde. Mudde argues that populism is a, "thin centered ideology that considers society to be separated into two homogenous and antagonistic groups, 'the pure people' versus 'the corrupt elite' and which argues that politics should be an expression of the general will of the people." Thin-centred refers to the concept that populism is more of a "symbiotic ideology" which requires a "host ideology." As such there is no such thing as a person who is only a populist, as it requires an ideology for populism to attach itself to, such as socialism, fascism, liberalism, conservatism, centrism, etc. Thus, rather than seeing those who are only populists, what is seen instead are socialist populists, fascist populists, liberal populists, etc. Likewise, the concept of popular sovereignty is closely linked with populism, and the attitude "of the people, by the people, for the people" is seen as justification for replacing politicians who are not properly representing the "pure people."

Another common feature of populism that has been noted by scholars is the prevalence of negative emotions such as distrust, dissatisfaction, and anger, with anger seeming to be the most widespread. Anger arises due to perceived harm or threat of harm from either the negligent or intentional actions administered by the elites, within the ideology of populism.

While the struggle for the people versus the elites is not unique within populist ideology, what separates populism from other ideologies, such as socialism, which sees the struggle in socio-economic terms, or nationalism, which views the antagonism within the context of the nation, is that populism is typically viewed within the context of morality. In other words, populist ideology sees the struggle between the people versus the elites as a struggle between good and evil. Thus, while compromise is generally seen as being central to benefiting all of society, populists typically see the elites as an existential threat. Consequently, the "will of the people" is viewed as being paramount to all political life, and liberal democratic institutions, such as rights, independent media, and the separation of powers, should not overrule the will of the people.

One final note on populism which deserves attention is the distinction between left-wing versus right-wing populism. Left-wing populism is typically characterized by upholding egalitarian and inclusive policies. Thus, left-wing populism extends rights to minorities, women, and other historically disenfranchised groups. Left-wing populism also typically envisions an idealized "heartland" that existed before an alleged "betrayal" of centre-left neoliberal policies. Whereas right-wing populism typically envisions the "pure people" in a more nativist context. With this being said, while there are a number of "social populist" parties within eastern Europe, who also hold anti-immigration stances, such as Robert Fico's SMER—Social Democracy in Slovakia, this anti-immigration stance is not central to their people versus the elite distinction, and thus does not fully fall into the category of right-wing populism.

Thus, it seems rather safe to conclude that the Narodniki exhibited many of the features of populism, with the exception of the prevalence of anger and the Manichean, good versus evil narrative. Yet, it does seem that the Narodnik movement upheld a strong moralistic and ethical stance, which will be explored further. Despite being a movement created by higher-class intellectuals, the Narodniki did favour the peasantry as being unique to Russia, and better than that of European capitalism [this will be elaborated on further]. The movement exhibited both Marxist and populist ideas, making the populism of the Narodniki a symbiotic ideology, as mentioned earlier. The emotion of anger doesn't seem to be present within the Narodniki, nor the concept of good versus evil, as the movement largely borrows from Marxist concepts of class struggle. Finally, while the Narodniki were a left-wing populist movement, they do not seem to envision an idealized heartland which was betrayed. While the movement was critical of the emancipation of the serfs as leading to a new form of wage slavery, they did not seem to argue that serfdom was, at any time, more desirable than the emancipation.

Also, it seems that unlike most populist movements, which followed, the Narodniki were unable to connect with their target populace, namely the peasantry. It seems that while appealing to the peasants' emotional dissatisfaction, the Narodniki were projecting outwards towards the peasants. Thus, the Narodniki seemed to hold the populist idea of, "I alone can fix it," but were not using the discourse that appeals to the masses.

Nevertheless, the Narodniki had a clear influence on the future of Russian politics. Most notably, the Bolshevik Revolution and the idea of Marxist-Leninism upheld that feudal societies could forgo capitalism and transition directly towards socialism.

Nikolay Konstantinovich Mikhaylovsky

The second part of this chapter will focus on one of the most important theoreticians of the Narodniki, Nikolay Mikhaylovsky. It will begin with a brief biography of his life and his role within the movement, as well as a brief overview of his ideas. Next, there will be a literature review comparing two sources, one regarding an in-depth analysis of his philosophy and the second being the competing theories as to how his life influenced his philosophy. Finally, it shall conclude with an analysis and critique of the thinker.

Nikolay Konstantinovich Mikhaylovsky, November 27 (O.S. November 15) 1842, Meshchovsk, – February 10 (O.S. January 28) 1904 Saint Petersburg was a Russian sociologist, literary critic, and publicist, who served as one of the key founders of an intellectual foundation for the Narodniki. Mikhaylovsky was born into a gentry-noble, but impoverished family. He was initially trained to become a mining engineer at the St. Petersburg Mining Institute. However, the young Mikhaylovsky was forced to drop out of his academic studies due to his support for Polish rebellions in 1863. From this point forward, Mikhaylovsky held numerous editorial positions, publishing for radical periodicals and various experimental entrepreneurial worker co-op positions. Initially influenced by the French anarchist philosopher Pierre-Joseph Proudhon, he translated many of his works into Russian. Yet, in 1868, Mikhaylovsky went on to establish himself within the periodical, *Otechestvennye zapiski* (Fatherland Notes), which would become the mouthpiece for the Narodnik movement.

Minor works within Mikhaylovsky's catalog included critiques of utilitarianism, with his works, "What is Happiness" and "Advocacy of the Emancipation of Women," which gained him widespread respect and acclaim from his fellow editors and publicists within the periodical, *Otechestvennye zapiski*. Following the death of the head of the periodical, Nikolay Nekrasov, in 1877, Mikhaylovsky became one of three co-editors and the de-facto head of *Otechestvennye zapiski*.

During this time, Mikhaylovsky was highly critical of social-Darwinism. In his essay, "What Is Progress?," Mikhaylovsky attacked what he saw among the social-Darwinists as the individual adapting to the environment for survival. Mikhaylovsky contended that the environment adapts to one's evolving personality. This evolution of social environments eventually leads to the struggle and emancipation of the individual for Mikhaylovsky. While highly critical of the social-Darwinists' stance of applying biological assumptions to social developmental theories, Mikhaylovsky countered these claims by asserting how organisms evolve from simple to complex (which he borrowed from Karl Ernst von Baer) and the principle of solidarity, which, at its core, social interaction fundamentally relies on cooperation.

Mikhaylovsky further elaborated on this critique by criticizing the division of labour within capitalist societies. This, he believed regressed humans as opposed to harmonious development and ultimately, the repression of individuality. Rather, Mikhaylovsky favoured a model similar to what he saw within the animal world, which emulated differentiation to progress such societies. Thus, he introduced an individualist outlook towards the Narodnik movement, which had previously been largely collective prior to Mikhaylovsky's involvement.

Another strikingly distinctive feature of Mikhaylovsky's thought was his views regarding social progress. Mikhaylovsky believed that all sociological theories must derive from a theoretical conception of utopianism. Mikhaylovsky's concept of a utopia involved the creation and development of a harmonious person. To Mikhaylovsky, cooperation, in its basic form, involved an egalitarian social group with solidarity as the chief principle of the society at hand. Yet, within societies with higher levels of complexity, with regard to cooperation, division of labour exists, in which the chief principle of these societies is the struggle for interconnectivity among egalitarian social groups. Thus, Mikhaylovsky concluded that a society can achieve an advanced level of development but maintain a lower level of organization. This is essentially how Mikhaylovsky saw capitalism and the division of labour within western European countries as opposed to peasantry within tsarist Russia. While western capitalist Europe was at a higher level of development, it was likewise at a lower level of organization, and vice versa within the peasant communities of tsarist Russia. Yet, Mikhaylovsky did favour moving towards a higher type of development, but in doing so, while preserving the higher level of organization.

Mikhaylovsky's main ideas regarding social change were further solidified with the development of the concept of the hero, or the Great Man theory, in relation to that of the crowd, or the people. The Great Man theory, which was the predominant discourse among intellectual circles of the 19th century, argues that the course of history and human events is shaped by that of an individual possessing unique characteristics and natural talents that set him apart from others, such as intellect, courage, charisma, etc. Mikhaylovsky challenged this idea in his 1882 essay, "Heroes of the Crowd," by arguing that a hero does not necessarily imply one with outstanding attributes regarding personality, but rather, through chance alone, finds himself as the leader of the crowd. Mikhaylovsky also emphasized that the leader can use both emotions and actions to reinforce the crowd, and in turn, the mass perception of the crowd can shape the role of the leader. To further elaborate on this concept, Mikhaylovsky also held that writers serve as moral judges of society, and the literature presented by such authors is an expression of the author's subjective standpoint in which the author situates himself.

While Mikhaylovsky took no part in violent revolutionary or illegal actions, his publications were highly provocative and often times openly called for the use of terroristic violent actions and the revolutionary over-throw of the tsar. Yet, Mikhaylovsky always maintained that it was the nobility's duty to advance the well-being of the peasantry and actively sought to distance himself from what he saw as the more vulgar characters of the populist movement. While facing growing political repression, Mikhaylovsky was temporarily banished from St Petersburg and the periodical was shut down. Following the assassination of Alexander II, Mikhaylovsky took part in addressing the People's Will Committee in an attempt to reposition the movement as a negotiating platform. Later, he took up an editing position in *Russkoye bogatstvo* ("Russian Wealth"), which upheld a more liberal stance with regard to populism. During this time, he became increasingly critical of the emerging Marxist movements as he saw them as harbouring industrialization and thus hindering the peasantry. He held this position until his death.

The next part of this chapter will focus on a literature review that provides a deeper understanding of Mikhaylovsky's thought. The article to be analyzed is titled, "Populism as a Philosophical Movement in Nineteenth-Century Russia: The Thought of P. L. Lavrov, and N. K. Mikhaylovsky" by James P. Scanlan. As this chapter is concerned with Mikhaylovsky, the aspects of philosophical thought regarding Lavrov will be ignored.

James P. Scanlan's work, "Populism as a Philosophical Movement in Nineteenth-Century Russia: The Thought of P. L. Lavrov, and N. K. Mikhaylovsky," Scanlan divides and examines the philosophy of each thinker into separate categories. These categories are metaphysics, epistemology, ethics, philosophy of history, social and political philosophy, and aesthetics. As mentioned before, this will only focus on the categories of philosophical thought with regards to Mikhaylovsky. Scanlan asserts that the Narodniki were influenced primarily by positivism, with regard to philosophy, and populism, with regard to social theory. Furthermore, Scanlan argues that the Narodniki were primarily motivated by reactionary politics in response to the ongoing social changes, with regards to the emancipation of the serfs. Thus, the Narodniki sought to position themselves in alignment with the legitimization of the communal traditions of the peasantry, in accordance with the morality of a future democratic socialist future for Russia. Thus, this philosophy of the Narodnik movement was essentially a Kantian version of positivism, akin to that of Auguste Comte, Proudhon, Hegel, and John Stewart Mill.

With regard to metaphysics, Mikhaylovsky rejected metaphysics because of the Kantian idea that only phenomena are accessible to humans and that the only knowledge one can gain of nature is through observation. Thus,

Mikhaylovsky subscribed to the philosophy of empiricism and agreed with John Stuart Mill's assertion that mathematical axioms are derived from generalized experiences. Yet, Mikhaylovsky did depart from positivism and empiricism by asserting that there were non-sensory phenomena, such as the interpretation of history, along with societies, norms, values, etc. Likewise, Mikhaylovsky acknowledged a phenomenon of consciousness that involved introspection of morality. Mikhaylovsky elaborated on this by arguing that the phenomenon of consciousness must be recognized as primary, since no other experience occurs apart from it. Thus, Mikhaylovsky referred to his social investigations as the "subjective method."

This so-called "subjective method" leads to Mikhaylovsky's epistemology. Scanlan argues that the epistemology employed by Mikhaylovsky amounts to a theoretical relativism which is equivalent to practical absolutism. Mikhaylovsky argues that "the satisfaction of cognitive need," as opposed to abstract truth, is the deciding factor for humans. Thus, Mikhaylovsky concludes that knowledge is relative only to that of the knower.

With regards to ethics, Mikhaylovsky emphasizes the use of the Russian term, "*pravda*," which combines both truth and justice. Furthermore, Mikhaylovsky argues that this is not only inseparable but also crucial for the combination of morality to determine the role of social inquiry. Thus, analysis within social sciences cannot be understood under objectivity and moral detachment. Yet, Scanlan notes that Mikhaylovsky is often times seen as being inconsistent within his ethical views. This is because, while Mikhaylovsky claims that morality is based on the "subjective method," he also states that moral claims are sought out in conformity to universal validity as opposed to personal choice. For Mikhaylovsky, this is the concept of the individual as the universal demand for human and societal evolution. Mikhaylovsky argues that this claim to individuality is rooted not only within the "subjective method" but also within objective science as well. Thus, Mikhaylovsky concludes that the value of social institutions is based on their promotion of individuality.

Mikhaylovsky's essay, "What Is Progress," deals with his philosophical views regarding historical development. Mikhaylovsky, once again, took up the "subjective method" of historical development. Moreover, Mikhaylovsky believed that history was contributed by individuals and interpreted by historians. "What Is Progress," as stated previously, is a critique of the social-Darwinist assumptions of combining scientific inquiry with that of historical inquiry. Mikhaylovsky disagreed with the claim that history leads to heterogeneity because of the notion of the simple evolving into the complex. Thus, for Mikhaylovsky, historical progress is the emancipation of the individual within society. Mikhaylovsky further critiqued the social-Darwinists by asserting that heterogeneity leads to the division of labour, which he agreed with Marx is detrimental to human development. Mikhaylovsky further developed his stages of history by assigning them teleological terms. The first stage is referred to as the *"objectively anthropocentric stage,"* which is a human-centred view regarding nature as having purposes to serve humanity. The next stage is *"eccentric (exocentric),"* which sees nature as being objective, but its parts are found equally across nature and not only among men. Finally, the last stage of historical development is the *"subjectively anthropocentric stage,"* which believes that purposes are not within nature, but are from man, and thus man gains supremacy over nature. Finally, as stated before, Mikhaylovsky rejects the evolutionary theory of social development, with regard to industrial societies being higher in development but lower in organization, as opposed to the peasantry, which was reversed.

Democratic socialism was seen as the best means to achieve individuality, according to Mikhaylovsky's social and political philosophy. Mikhaylovsky favoured economic cooperation as a means of achieving egalitarianism, which he believed would be best suited for agrarian socialism. These would be facilitated by the use of peasant village communes and production cooperation. Yet, Mikhaylovsky was subject to censorship under the tsarist regime and thus could not speak freely of revolutions. Though he did eventually give his approval to terroristic activities and other acts of violence. While Mikhaylovsky was an admirer of Karl Marx, he was more influenced by his critiques of capitalism, as opposed to his solutions of industrialized socialism and communism. Mikhaylovsky was also against the organic theory of the state, arguing that consciousness is derived from individuals as opposed to groups. This critique, from Mikhaylovsky, would not only be levied against the social-Darwinists, but also against Marx and his views of societies and individuals as well.

Mikhaylovsky championed the idea of aesthetics as being fundamental to an individual's creative impulse. Yet, he also believed that art should serve moral and ethical standards for society. Thus, Mikhaylovsky was against the concept of "art for art's sake" and rather promoted the artistic movement of social realism. His view of art was that it should serve society by promoting the positive ideals of society as a whole, as opposed to a certain social class. Much like his view of the author being a spokesperson for society, Mikhaylovsky contended that an artist and the critic were to employ the "subjective method" in which the artist must speak to the inner lives of the audience and the critic must speak to the relationship between the artist and his subject.

Analysis and critique

As Scanlan pointed out, Mikhaylovsky was a sociologist as opposed to a philosopher. Thus, inconsistencies within his ideological worldview need to be understood not as a shortcoming of his philosophy as a whole, but as a result of his approach to philosophy, which was that of a sociologist. Yet, a main critique seems to be his efforts to objectify his so-called "subjective method" through positivism and biology. Thus, it seems he was doing the reverse of the social-Darwinists, he was trying to critique, in an attempt to falsify their philosophy on their level.

This can also be seen with his version of the hero and the Great Man theory. Rather than trying to disprove the theory or provide an alternative, he seems to provide a different perspective on an old idea. This seems to be a means to rationalize his philosophy, within an existing paradigm, at the time, to make it more accessible to the masses.

It seems that this can also be reflected in the efforts made by the Narodniki with regards to the peasants. The movement tried to communicate on the same level as that of the peasants, but ultimately failed to convert them. Thus, it seems that while Mikhaylovsky was able to create unique ideas and in-depth philosophical insights, he was not able to create a philosophy that was radically different from those he was ideologically opposed to, and thus was unable to persuade those around him. This lack of a radically new philosophical insight can be seen in his later life, after the assassination of Alexander II, by acting as a negotiator with the regime.

It also seems that Mikhaylovsky was quite unsure of a precise vision for the future with regards to Russia and the peasants. While he did favour expanding Russian development while maintaining peasant organization, it doesn't seem clear what this development would entail. This opaque view is rather similar to Martin Heidegger's perspective on technology, who stated that he was not against technology, as it allowed a means of uncovering; yet all of his actions and writings strongly suggest that he is against technology.

Thus, it seems that Mikhaylovsky's largest short coming was not from philosophical or ideological inconsistency, but rather the fear of becoming too radical, and thus trying to balance the revolutionary with the normative aspects of his philosophy. With this being said, his theories are, nonetheless, unique and helped provide new ways of looking at old concepts. While he was a forerunner in populism, and the Narodniki being the first modern populist movement, it seems that this is also evident within the populist movement he helped create. The Narodniki, much like Mikhaylovsky, were attempting to provide a new perspective on old ideas, that is Marxism and Russian peasantry, without radically altering the two. This also seems to be a common trend with the numerous populist movements that would soon follow, even to this day, with regards to new perspectives on older ideas.

Bibliography

Abramowitz, A. The Great Alignment: Race, Party Transformation, and the Rise of Donald Trump. New Haven, CT: Yale University Press, 2018.

Billington, James H. Mikhailovsky and Russian Populism. Oxford: Clarendon Press, 1958.

Britannica The Editors of Encyclopaedia. "Nikolay Konstantinovich Mikhaylovsky." Encyclopedia Britannica, *Invalid Date*. https://www.britannica.com/biography/Nikolay-Konstantinovich-Mikhaylovsky.

Edie, James M., James P. Scanlan, and M. B. Zeldin, eds. Russian Philosophy. Vol. 2. Chicago, IL: Quadrangle Books, 1965.

Efemenko, D., and Y. Evseeva. "Studies of Social Solidarity in Russia: Tradition and Modern Trends." American Sociologist 43, no. 4 (2012): 349–365.

Field, Daniel. Peasants and Propagandists in the Russian Movement to the People in 1874. London: Garland, 1992.

Figes, Orlando. A People's Tragedy: The Russian Revolution, 1891–1924. London: Jonathan Cape, 1996.

Figes, Orlando. *Crimea: The Last Crusade.* London: Allen Lane, 2010.

Frierson, Cathy A. *Peasant Icons: Representations of Rural People in Late 19th Century Russia.* New York: Oxford University Press, 1993.

Glinski, Dimitri. "Mikhailovsky, Nikolai Konstantinovich." Encyclopedia of Russian History. Encyclopedia.com. October 3, 2022. https://www.encyclopedia.com/history/encyclopedias-almanacs-transcripts-and-maps/mikhailovsky-nikolai-konstantinovich

Grinin, Leonid. "The Role of an Individual in History: A Reconsideration." Social Evolution & History 9, no. 2 (2010): 95–136.

Hofstadter, R. "The Paranoid Style in American Politics." *Harpers Magazine*, 1964.

Hooghe, M., and S. Marien. "A Comparative Analysis of the Relation between Political Trust and Forms of Political Participation in Europe." European Studies 14 (2012): 1–18.

Ivanov-Razumnik, R.I. Istoria russkoi obshchestvennoi mysli. Vol. 2. Moscow: Respublika, Terra, 1997, pp. 228–302.

Lavrov, and N. K. Mikhajlovskij. "Lavrov and N. K. Mikhajlovskij." Studies in Soviet Thought 27, no. 3 (1984): 209. http://www.jstor.org/stable/20099320

Mansbridge, Jane, and Stephan Macedo. "Populism and Democratic Theory." Annual Review of Law and Social Science 15, no. 1 (2019, October 13): 59–77. https://doi.org/10.1146/annurev-lawsocsci-101518-042843

March, Luke. "From Vanguard of the Proletariat to Vox Populi: Left-Populism as a 'Shadow' of Contemporary Socialism." SAIS Review 27, no. 1 (2007): 63–77.

March, Luke. Radical Left Parties in Europe. New York: Routledge, 2011.

Maxwell, Margaret. Narodniki Women: Russian Women Who Sacrificed Themselves for the Dream of Freedom. Oxford: Pergamon Press, 1990.

Mee, Arthur, J. A. Hammerton, and Arthur D. Innes. Harmsworth History of the World: Volume 7. London: Carmelite House, 1907, p. 5193.

Mikhaylovsky, N. K. Heroes and Crowd: Collected Works in Sociology. 2 vols. St. Petersburg: Aleteya, 1998.

Miller, Warren E. "Disinterest, Disaffection, and Participation in Presidential Politics." Political Behavior 2, no. 1 (1980): 7–32.

Moon, David. The Abolition of Serfdom in Russia, 1762–1907. Harlow, England: Pearson Education, 2001. pp. 49–55.

Mudde, Cas, and Cristóbal Rovira Kaltwasser. Brève Introduction au Populisme. La Tour d'Aigues: Fondation Jean-Jaurès, 2018.

Pearl, Deborah. "The People's Will." In Encyclopedia of Russian History, edited by James R. Millar, 1162–1163. New York: Thomson Gale, 2003, pp. 1162–1163.

Pipes, Richard. "Narodnichestvo: A Semantic Inquiry." Slavic Review 23, no. 3 (1964): 441–58. https://doi.org/10.2307/2492683.

Pipes, Richard. Russia Under the Old Regime. New York: Collier Books, 1992.

Polunov, Alexander, Thomas C. Owen, and L. G. Zakharova. Russia in the Nineteenth Century: Autocracy, Reform, and Social Change, 1814–1914. Translated by Marshall S. Shatz. Armonk, NY: M. E. Sharpe, 2005.

Pushkarev, Sergei G. "The Russian Peasants' Reaction to the Emancipation of 1861." Russian Review 27, no. 2 (April 1968): 199–214. https://doi.org/10.2307/127028

Scanlan, James P. "Populism as a Philosophical Movement in Nineteenth-Century Russia: The Thought of P. L. Lavrov and N. K. Mikhajlovskij." Studies in Soviet Thought 27, no. 3 (1984): 209–223. http://www.jstor.org/stable/20099320.

Tankaka, Masaharu. "The Narodniki and Marx on Russian Capitalism in the 1870s–1880s." Kyoto University Economic Review 39, no. 2 (87) (1969): 1–25. http://www.jstor.org/stable/43217169.

Tocal, M., and J. R. Montero. Political Disaffection in Contemporary Democracies: Social Capital, Institutions, and Politics, Democratization. Abingdon: Routledge, 2006.

Ulam, Adam B. In the Name of the People: Prophets and Conspirators in Prerevolutionary Russia. New York: Putnam, 1977.

Vasilopoulou, S., and M. Wagner. "Fear, Anger and Enthusiasm about the EU: Effects of Emotional Reactions on Public Preferences Towards European Integration." European Union Politics 18, no. 3 (2017): 382–405.

Venturi, Franco. "Chaikovskists and Movement 'To Go To The People.'" In Roots of Revolution. London: Weidenfeld and Nicolson, 1960, pp. 62–70.

Venturi, Franco. Roots of Revolution. Rev. ed. Translated by Francis Haskell. London: Phoenix Press, 2001.

Von Laue, Theodore H. "The Fate of Capitalism in Russia: The Narodnik Version." American Slavic and East European Review 13, no. 1 (1954): 11–28. https://doi.org/10.2307/2492162

Walicki, A. The Controversy Over Capitalism: Studies in the Social Philosophy of the Russian Populists. Oxford: Clarendon Press, 1969.

Wetherell, Charles, and Andrejs Plakans. "Borders, Ethnicity, and Demographic Patterns in the Russian Baltic Provinces in the Late Nineteenth Century." Continuity and Change 14 (1999): 33–56.

6

THE MORAL DOCTRINE AND EPISTEMIC SPHERE OF VLADIMIR SOLOVYOV

Feeza Vasudeva

Introduction

Vladimir Sergeevich Solovyov (1853–1900) is considered one of the most prolific and influential philosophers of the nineteenth-century Russian Empire. He has even been considered one of the first systematic philosophers of Russia (Motroshilova 2021). While his metaphysical commitments have sometimes marginalized his reception in Western philosophical circles, particularly due to the modernist privileging of epistemology over metaphysics, Solovyov's project constitutes an attempt to reconcile rational inquiry with spiritual insight. However, his veritable system of thought in the shape of free-rational thought influenced many thinkers. As Motroshilova (2021) has argued, Solovyov was among the first Russian thinkers to deliberately extend philosophical reasoning across these traditionally demarcated spheres of philosophy, theology, ontology, epistemology, and even politics, thereby transforming the Russian intellectual discourse. However, these claims also bear scrutiny and invite us to ask how one might distinguish a critical appropriation of Solovyov's work from echoing these grand claims, and if it is possible to extract a critical moral philosophy from a thinker so deeply shaped by metaphysical and religious concerns?

This chapter engages precisely with such questions by offering a focused analysis of Solovyov's moral philosophy—specifically, the idea of an objective moral essence as articulated in *Justification of the Moral Good* (*Opravdanie dobra* 1897). Rather than simply reiterating existing appraisals, this study interrogates the internal coherence of Solovyov's moral system and its autonomy from his broader metaphysical framework. In doing so, it diverges from interpretations like that of Evgenii Trubetskoi, who

DOI: 10.4324/9781003541004-7

emphasized the inseparability of Solovyov's ethics from his religious metaphysics and aligns more closely with scholars such as Simons (1999), who contend that Solovyov's moral thought seeks a "comparative autonomy" from dogmatic theology and positive religion.

Thus, this chapter pursues two principal aims: first, to trace the genesis of Solovyov's moral philosophy within the context of his evolving metaphysical and epistemological commitments; and second, it seeks to understand how Solovyov's moral sphere coincides with his epistemic sphere. Before examining the moral essence of Solovyov's thought, it is essential to explore the genesis of his ideas. Solovyov's work cannot be categorized as secular, as it is deeply influenced by biblical thought. Even a cursory reading of his works reveals the nature of this influence. However, this shouldn't lead us to completely disregard his scholarship. Solovyov's work also demonstrates an effort to rationally preserve specific positions that have often been superficially understood as a matter of religion and, hence, extra-philosophical.

Subsequently, the chapter turns to Solovyov's moral theory proper, emphasizing his efforts to assert the independence of moral philosophy from metaphysics and epistemology. It will also address his views on moral foundations. The final sections of the chapter address Solovyov's epistemological framework, especially his conception of "knowledge" and "philosophy," to elucidate how these categories underpin his vision of moral philosophy. Ultimately, the chapter will argue that Solovyov's ethics should not be viewed as merely derivative of his metaphysics, but rather as a semi-autonomous domain within his broader philosophical vision—one that seeks to bridge, rather than subordinate, the moral and the metaphysical.

A brief genesis—Vladimir Solovyov's thought

Born on January 16, 1853, into a devout Christian family, Solovyov was raised in a household deeply rooted in the traditions of the Russian Orthodox Church. His father, a distinguished historian and lecturer at the University of Moscow, was a devoted believer. In his lifetime, Solovyov claimed to have experienced three mystical visions, which he penned down in his autobiographical poem "Three Meetings," and which were instrumental in shaping his life and philosophical understandings (Solovyov 1990). These mystical episodes served not merely as personal religious experiences but as formative metaphysical events. They confirmed for Solovyov the real presence of the divine within the world and the possibility of a reconciled universal harmony and divine integration—ideas that would crystallize in his doctrine of *vseedinstvo* or All-Unity (Smith 2010). In the first vision, occurring when he was just nine years old, he experienced an overwhelming sense of the divine feminine presence during prayer in a church. The second, which occurred in 1875 while he was studying in London, took place in the British Museum, where he claimed to once again perceive Sophia as a living, radiant presence. In response to this encounter, he abruptly left for Egypt where, in the desert, he again experienced the apparition of Sophia, confirming his vocation to work for the unification of spiritual truths.

These visions, steeped in mystical symbolism, catalyzed a lifelong search for intellectual and spiritual synthesis—one that began to take philosophical form during his studies at the University of Moscow. There, Solovyov recognized the need for a philosophy that was not merely critical or analytical, but one that offered positive metaphysical content (Sutton 1988). Among his early and enduring influences was Baruch Spinoza, whose pantheistic metaphysics—especially the notion of *positive total-unity* and the rational order of the cosmos—played a crucial role in guiding Solovyov towards a reconciliation between reason and religious faith (Zenkovsky 2003a). This mutual immanence between material and immaterial was, for Solovyov, a crucial step towards metaphysical integration. Yet Spinoza's impersonal substance was not the end point of Solovyov's inquiry, who believed that the absence of a mediating principle that could make the unity of spirit and matter concrete rendered Spinoza's monism insufficient. The rigid separation of *natura naturans* and *natura naturata*, though conceptually unified, offered no pathway for real interaction or transformation between soul and body. Solovyov was striving not merely for metaphysical parallelism but for a "middle term" a real principle of integration (Smith 2010, 38).

Solovyov's philosophical development was also shaped by German thinkers, yet his engagement was critical and selective, and his orientation remained distinctively theistic. From Schelling and even Böhme, he adopted the notion of a living cosmos imbued with divine life, yet his doctrine of Divine Humanity (*Theandry*) surpassed theirs in emphasizing the metaphysical centrality of Man. For Solovyov, the human being is not merely a reflection of the Absolute, but its coeternal content—freely united with God and capable of redeeming the cosmos through voluntary self-surrender (Kojève 2018, 43). Solovyov also engaged with Kant, whom he saw as both foundational and limited. As Smerdov (2002) notes, Solovyov appreciated Kant's emphasis on the subjective nature of knowledge and the problem of "one-sidedness" in modern philosophy. However, he resisted Kant's separation between phenomena and noumena, which he saw as perpetuating a disjunction between the human and the divine. Solovyov sought a metaphysical unity that could account not only for epistemological integrity but for real, lived union between the spiritual and the material. The post-Kantian tradition likewise shaped him: Fichte's expansion of transcendental subjectivity, and Hartmann's unconscious metaphysics, were both acknowledged but ultimately redirected towards a personalist metaphysics. Hegel, while influential in terms of dialectical method, was rejected for his abstract absolutism that dissolved God into history. For Solovyov, unlike Hegel or Comte, Man could not replace God—he could only be "absolute" in and through union with the divine (Kline 1974). This delicate balance of exalted human freedom and divine primacy reveals Solovyov's attempt to reconcile German philosophical rigor with Christian metaphysical depth (Smith 2010; Kojève 2018).

Upon graduating at the age of 18, Solovyov decided to pursue further study at the Moscow Theological Academy. This was an unconventional move in an intellectual climate dominated by positivism and the natural sciences, which many among the intelligentsia deemed more respectable than theology. However, his thesis titled "The Crisis of Western Philosophy" or "*Krizis zapadnoy filosofii*," garnered much praise, leading him to be offered a position at Moscow University. His public lectures, particularly the series on *Godmanhood* (*Bogochelovechestvo*) delivered in 1881, attracted wide attention and were attended by notable figures such as Fyodor Dostoevsky and Leo Tolstoy. During the subsequent years (during which he was also forced to resign from his lectureship), Solovyov devoted himself to theological and metaphysical reflection, seeking to heal the schisms within Christian thought and between Eastern and Western traditions. Finally, after much sojourn during which he travelled to Britain and even Egypt (based on his vision from the mystical being Sophia), he returned to Russia to explore the complexities of philosophical thought.

Solovyov's intellectual development can broadly be divided into three distinct stages. The first phase was marked by metaphysical-mystical preoccupations, while the second period was devoted to critical writing. In his final period, Solovyov returned to mystical themes, but now with a more deliberate effort to synthesize diverse philosophical and theological traditions into a coherent metaphysical system. His thought, therefore, was neither static nor strictly linear; it evolved in complexity and purpose. While his mystical inclinations often led critics to dismiss him as eccentric or even heretical, scholars have emphasized the enduring philosophical and theological significance of his later works (Smith 2010). Even the great Indian humanist Rabindranath Tagore, during his visit to the Soviet Union, asserted,

> I'll want to view the land of Tolstoy, Dostoevsky and Solovyov...The great Russian people, which created values of the spirit that are a contribution to the treasury of world civilization...is now on the way to a great future.
> *(Golubev 1978)*

For a variety of reasons, it was in the later years of his life that Solovyov turned once again to questions of moral and theoretical philosophy. For him, theoretical inquiry—while irreducible to other domains—was inseparable from and ultimately subordinate to moral considerations. As he writes,

In the domain of moral ideas philosophy, despite its formal autonomy, is essentially subordinated to the vital interests of the pure will, which strives for the good and requires from reason a clear and complete explanation as to the nature of authentic good...

(Solovyov 1996 [1897]).

It is during this period that he produced one of his most significant works entitled *Justification of the Good* or *Opravdanie dobra,* which concerned itself with the emendation and reformulation of moral philosophy. Here, Solovyov showcased how moral philosophy finds association with religiosity in its essence but with theoretical philosophy in respect of cognitive method. For Solovyov, the task of theoretical philosophy was not to create new moral systems but to discern and articulate the inner truth of those already given. Theoretical philosophy, in this respect, has an objective purview—dealing with structures of knowledge and reality—whereas moral philosophy is subjective, directed towards inner experience (Simons 1999). Solovyov's later works are also intended to asseverate the idea of Good and to showcase how this acquiescence to Good is not merely about passive resistance to evil (contra Tolstoy). It is also during this period that he sought an organic synthesis of religion, philosophy, and science in the interests of an integral life, a synthesis that aimed not only at theoretical coherence but also at the realization of a morally Good life (Gubman 1993). This endeavour reflected Solovyov's aspiration to restore an "organic view of the universe," one that countered the increasing fragmentation of knowledge in modernity (Obolevitch 2020). Although his untimely death prevented us from witnessing the full maturation of this integrative vision, his later writings indicate a sustained effort to achieve a synthetic unity across disciplinary boundaries. Importantly, Solovyov did not aim to create new specialized disciplines in isolation; rather, he proposed a framework that embraced "the multiplicity, the multidimensionality of a systematic approach" to knowledge and human existence (Motroshilova 2021, 165).

Solovyov's moral computations

In the early pages of his magnum opus, *Justification*, Solovyov writes,

The object of this book for all who resolve to follow it is to show *the good as truth*, i.e., as the one correct path that is true to itself and is to be followed on all occasions in life and to the end. I mean the Moral Good *in its essence*. It and only it justifies itself and justifies our trust in it.

(Solovyov 1996 [1897], li)

From an early stage in his philosophical work, Solovyov engages deeply with the concepts of "good" and "truth," placing them at the heart of moral inquiry. For Solovyov, the notion of the Good is inextricably linked to moral essence and is not merely an ethical ideal but the central focus of moral philosophy itself. He maintains that moral philosophy must function as a rational discourse aimed at transforming human will in alignment with the Good. This rationality connects it to both religion and theoretical philosophy. It is in his concerns with the notions of Good, truth and even knowledge that his philosophy seeks to reintroduce an element of transcendentalism (Swiderski 1999).

Despite his strong religious convictions, Solovyov was critical of grounding moral philosophy solely on metaphysics, which manifests itself as religion, or in epistemology, which is the theory of knowledge. He argued that such foundations risk subordinating the moral sphere to external systems of authority, thereby stripping it of its inherent content and autonomy. Moral philosophy, he insisted, must preserve its independence precisely because metaphysical systems often embed morality within historically contingent forms—such as churches, institutions, and nations—that obscure its universal essence. In this sense, Solovyov offers a critique of religious dogmatism: any individual who uncritically submits to external moral authority without recognizing his subjective involvement in that submission lapses into absurdity.

In Solovyov's philosophical framework, external authority, whether religious, institutional, or political, is not regarded as an ultimate or immutable source of moral law, but rather as a historically necessary stage in humanity's moral development. It functions as a provisional guide that must eventually yield to a higher synthesis grounded in the unity of faith, reason, and lived experience. True moral Good, in Solovyov's view, cannot be externally imposed; it must be freely affirmed through a convergence of personal consciousness, rational insight, and spiritual intuition. This vision integrates his theological commitment to Christian revelation with a philosophical pursuit of truth and ethical autonomy, forming what he calls a morally worthy condition of existence (Solovyov 1996 [1897], lxii–lxiv).

Yet, we are presented here with a new dilemma, one that concerns itself with "moral *amorphism* or *subjectivism*" which "reduces everything to us alone, to our self-consciousness and autonomy" (Solovyov 1996 [1897], lxiv, emphasis in original). This means the disavowal of all religious and sociopolitical life in a historical sense. However, for Solovyov, if all matters of historicity and its manifestations are denied, and history is reduced to an arbitrator of norms, then there can be no organic evolution of history and historical processes. He disagrees with such a view, which, contra Christian faith, makes him more accepting of the Darwinian theory of evolution (Sládek 2010). Here, Solovyov is also arguing against the Hegelian tradition. In contrast to Hegel's dialectical idealism, which interprets history as the self-realization of Spirit, where being is always in the process of becoming, Solovyov posits a boundary between history and being. For him, history does not exhaust the essence of being, nor does it possess intrinsic teleological finality. Instead, history provides the conditions through which moral consciousness may emerge, but it is not itself the origin or determinant of moral truth (Navickas 1966). It is this perspective that also makes Solovyov more open to Darwinian evolutionary theory. While many Christian thinkers rejected evolution for its seemingly materialist implications, Solovyov saw in it a natural, albeit incomplete, expression of divine order and progression, compatible with his vision of moral and spiritual development (Sládek 2010). Ultimately, Solovyov's approach calls for a synthesis: one that neither reduces morality to subjective autonomy nor to historical or institutional authority alone. Instead, he emphasizes a dynamic interplay between the individual and history, the spiritual and the rational.

Building on this dialectical tension between subjective moral autonomy and historical authority, Solovyov identifies two symmetrical moral fallacies. On the one hand, there is the uncritical submission to history, understood as external authority—be it the Church, the state, or cultural tradition—treated as if inherently Good. On the other hand, there is the complete rejection of all historical forms as corrupt or inherently evil, a position that collapses into moral nihilism or radical subjectivism. While these positions may appear antithetical, Solovyov reveals their deeper congruence: both fail to grasp the Good in its essential, unconditional nature. As he writes:

> The two opposing views agree that neither takes the good *in its essence*, as the good itself is. Both connect the good with acts and relationships that can be either good or evil depending on what inspired them and the goal they serve. In other words, something good, but which can become evil, is substituted for the Good, and the conditional is taken as unconditional.
> *(Solovyov 1996 [1897], lxvii, emphasis in original)*

In the first view, the externality in the form of institutions is viewed as unconditionally good, moral, or revered, or in the latter view, the externality is completely rejected as evil. Solovyov, however, insists that the true Good must be distinguished by its absoluteness and unconditioned universality. It cannot be reduced to any temporal form or subjective expression, yet it cannot be realized apart from them. Instead, the Good must serve as the very condition of moral life itself—the measure by which both history and autonomy are judged, not the other way around. This is where its purity lies, and where Solovyov's doctrine of All-Unity finds ethical expression: the Good as the unifying ground that transcends and integrates both the individual and the historical.

The notion of all-unity or total-unity is important in Solovyov's work. First developed in *The Philosophical Principles of Integral Knowledge* and elaborated across his later works, all-unity was conceived not merely as a metaphysical abstraction but as a principle with moral and historical significance. Solovyov contended that humanity is not the passive object of history but its active, collective subject. As he puts it, "the subject of the historical process is mankind as a whole, real, and collective organism" (Solovyov as cited in Navickas 1966, n.p.). This metaphysical unity, which transcends individualism, becomes for Solovyov a fundamental basis of moral doctrine, which then comes to the absolute Good.

Kant's separation of the Good's purity from its universality, Solovyov believed, resulted in a detachment from the moral content needed to realize the Good in actual life. Solovyov's notion of the Good, by contrast, is both rational and unifying—it requires completeness, not mere autonomy. Reflecting on other philosophical traditions, he remarked:

In this context, Solovyov's position diverges sharply from Immanuel Kant's. While recognizing the merit of Kantian doctrine and accrediting him as the father of moral philosophy, he remained critical of what he saw as Kant's abstract subjectivism. Kant's separation of the Good's purity from its universality, Solovyov believed, resulted in a detachment from the moral content needed to realize the Good in actual life. Solovyov's notion of the Good, by contrast, is both rational and unifying—it requires completeness, not mere autonomy. Reflecting on German philosophical traditions, he remarked:

> I obtained.. not dialectical moments of an abstract idea (as in Hegel) nor empirical complications of natural facts (as in Herbert Spencer), but the completeness of moral norms for all fundamental practical relations of our individual and collective life...Only such completeness justifies the good in our consciousness, and only on the condition of such completeness can the moral good realize for us its purity and its invincible strength.
>
> *(Solovyov 1996 [1897], lxx)*

This brings us to the question: what, according to Solovyov, are the foundations of a morally good life? He finds the answer in the experiences or feelings of shame, pity, and reverence (*reverentia*) (ibid.). An awareness of these feelings, for Solovyov, is independent of a metaphysical experience and an inherent part of human nature. Unlike Darwin or Schopenhauer, Solovyov does not view these feelings as products of evolutionary adaptation or utilitarian calculation. Instead, they are irreducible expressions of our moral relation to the world. Shame, in particular, functions as a means of distinguishing the human from the merely natural. It signals a break from instinct and a recognition of one's higher moral vocation.

This framework resonates strongly with anthropological theories on the dynamics of guilt and shame in cultural systems. The distinction between "guilt cultures" and "shame cultures," developed by anthropologists such as Benedict (1946) and Creighton (1990), offers a useful lens here. In such models, shame is often associated with external social judgement and relational identity, while guilt is linked to internalized moral law. Solovyov's privileging of shame as a morally foundational experience suggests a model that synthesizes both: shame reflects our awareness of deviation from an ideal moral image (as in shame cultures), yet it is internalized and connected to spiritual conscience (as in guilt cultures). This internal-external fusion highlights Solovyov's broader philosophical commitment to integration and all-unity.

In addition to shame, pity grounds our moral relation to others by affirming the value of our moral relation to other living forms. And while feelings of shame and pity put us in relation to what is lower and what is equal to us, the feeling of reverence puts us in relation to what is supreme. The latter, in this sense, becomes a spiritual relation. Here, we are again made acquainted with his theological preference when he equates the feelings of reverence with the "eternally existent" or God. He writes:

> In the two moral spheres indicated by shame and pity, the moral good is already known to be the truth and is realized in reality, albeit only imperfectly. In the third sphere of moral relations, viz., the one determined by a religious feeling, or reverence, the true object of such a feeling reveals itself to be the highest or perfect moral good, not just being realized but unconditionally and fully realized, i.e., the eternal existent.
>
> *(Creighton 1990, 144)*

Thus, amongst the three, he gives preference to the feeling of reverence, which for him constitutes the ultimate moral Good. He offers no strict rational deduction for this ordering; rather, it is presented as a given, intuitive structure of human moral experience. This position leads him to diverge from Kant once more. Where Kant posited God as a postulate of practical reason, necessary for the coherence of moral law but epistemically inaccessible, Solovyov insists on the immediacy of divine reality in human moral life. For him, faith is not supplementary to reason but a constitutive element of moral knowledge itself (Kant 1956 [1788]).

Solovyov's reflections on moral life do not end with the triad of shame, pity, and reverence. He further elaborates on the structure of religious feeling by identifying three interrelated elements that accompany it. These include "a negative attitude towards the present," followed by a "positive aspiration towards the higher ideal," and finally "an aspiration to change oneself" in conjunction with a higher ideal (Nemeth 2015, xli). These elements point to an inherently transformative impulse within the moral-religious life, echoing what Solovyov frames as a categorical imperative: "not only *to desire perfection*, but *to be perfect*" (Solovyov 1996 [1897], 149, emphasis in original). Solovyov recognizes that attaining perfection is not an easy task but a lifelong one, and that this task of perfection denotes the full scope of moral Good.

This raises a deeper question: if shame, pity, and reverence are foundational to our moral experience, and if they manifest as conditions of a fundamental moral being, then what kind of world must humans be in? Here, Solovyov turns to the question of value itself and its relation to empirical inquiry. He acknowledges the importance of empirical investigations even within the disciplines of biology, anthropology, etc. Yet he insists that such empirical pursuits must remain anchored within a broader metaphysical framework. As Swiderski notes, Solovyov sees these empirical studies as meaningful "only in order to elucidate the ontic foundations of values and their conditions of realization" (Swiderski 1999, 204). In other words, for Solovyov, underneath the values of pity, reverence, and shame there is an objectivity to the moral order that requires an active participation from the subject involving cognitive states of reasoning. Thus, while Solovyov's philosophical project remains deeply metaphysical, it is never divorced from the cognitive and epistemic dimensions of human life. He resists moral dogmatism not by abandoning religious foundations, but by integrating them within a framework of philosophical inquiry that includes epistemology and metaphysics. It is this integration that characterizes the distinctiveness of his thought. The following section, therefore, turns to an examination of Solovyov's epistemological sphere.

Solovyov's epistemic sphere: theory of knowledge

Solovyov's engagement with the epistemic sphere is most clearly articulated in his *Philosophical Principles of Integral Knowledge* and the posthumously incomplete *Theoretical Philosophy*. The latter was left unfinished due to his early death. His theory of knowledge had diverse inspirations, from Plato to German philosophy, particularly that of Schopenhauer as well as Schelling.

For Solovyov, the pursuit of a theory of knowledge is inseparable from the nature and function of philosophy itself. He argued that "in the abstract, purely theoretical knowledge has completed its development and passed irrevocably into history" (Zenkovsky 2003b, 487). Philosophy for him could only have relative independence, while presuming it as a function of the religious sphere (ibid). Although he does not extensively elaborate on the nature of this relative independence, he is clear that philosophy, in isolation, fails to fulfil any meaningful task. His focus, on the contrary, is on the amalgamation of theology, science and philosophy which will provide us with an integral knowledge that can be combined with an integral society i.e. "the unity of the spiritual, political and economic societies" (Nemeth 2019, 76). This in turn leads to integral life i.e. "the correlated activity of the various organs" that constitute a general sphere (ibid). As Solovyov writes:

> Only when man's will and intellect enter into communion with that which eternally and truly is, will all the particular forms and elements of life and knowledge take on positive meaning and value, becoming the necessary organs of a single integral life.
>
> *(As quoted in Zenkovsky 2003b, 488)*

While advancing his theory of knowledge, Solovyov identified four approaches (Shein 1970). The first two are empiricism and rationalism. While recognizing their merit, Solovyov believed that they could be peremptory in their surety of cognizing reality. Empiricism, in Solovyov's view, suffers from a fundamental tension: it presumes the subjectivity of thought and the objectivity of experience, thus reducing truth to what remains once subjective elements are stripped away and experience is fully objectified. However, Solovyov argues that experience itself can be divided into two components—external and internal. For Solovyov, empiricism focuses on externality while rejecting that the truth itself can be in the internal experience of the one who is cognizing. Similarly, rationalism, which places its epistemic confidence in the powers of reason, as typified by Descartes and Kant, ultimately leads to an abstraction that alienates the subject. For Solovyov, this fails to reflect the actual structure of cognition. He writes that "cognition is cognition of objects, which presupposes both subjective and objective elements" (Shein 1970, 3). Therefore, any epistemology that neglects the co-presence of both poles falls short of a comprehensive account of knowledge.

Solovyov recognizes the third approach to be skepticism, which he promptly dismisses by asserting that it employs rationality to shatter reason. Finally, he believes the fourth approach to be the most substantial one and the one that can give us true knowledge, i.e., the one that employs mystical intuition. For Solovyov, abstract thinking is based on the thought that the world is my idea. Solovyov has borrowed Schelling's notion of the world as an idea *(Vorstellung)* and the fact that the mind has a significant place in the cognizing process. Branches such as science, theology, and philosophy seek to interpret ideas, while rationality seeks to verify knowledge and not generate it. It is only religious or mystical knowledge that is true, for "our logical thinking acquires its unconditional rationality, and our experience the significance of unconditional reality, only from this perception"

(Zenkovsky 2003b, 520). Here, Solovyov is trying to disavow the thought of epistemological immanentism, while arguing that the criteria of truth are situated outside of the colonizer, while being independent of an external object. The question of how mystical knowledge is brought about is unanswered. Solovyov does assert that it is not mystical knowledge alone that leads to integral knowledge but a synthesis of theology, science, and philosophy. Furthermore, for him, mysticism, in combination with empiricism and rationalism, must present us with the true basis of philosophy (Zenkovsky 2003b, 519).

In his works, Solovyov does differentiate between integral and abstract knowledge. While reason and logic are means of asserting knowledge that is intuitive, he maintains that in the act of knowing "we have something more than what is given in our sensations and concepts" (Shein 1970, 8). Thus, the cognition of an object takes place in a twofold manner—in the initial stage, it is external and then internal from the reference point of absolute being which is mystical and therefore, absolute knowledge. This internal knowledge, which can also synthesize subject and object, finds its expression in "faith, imagination and creativity," and their synthesis is "the *sine qua non* for a genuine knowledge of reality" as well as being the principal task of philosophy (Shein 1970, 9). However, this further brings us to the question, how does the moral Good feature in Solovyov's theoretical philosophy and within his epistemic sphere? The next section explores that.

Moral good and theoretical philosophy

In developing the first principle of his theoretical philosophy, Solovyov argued that philosophy is uniquely positioned to illuminate the true nature of the moral Good (Nemeth 2019). For him, the pursuit of truth and the pursuit of the Good are not separate endeavours but fundamentally the same. Yet this moral quest requires a corresponding epistemological framework. Hence, here we see Solovyov's attempt to bring his reflections on theoretical philosophy, moral philosophy, and theology together to understand the objective validity of the object, particularly the moral essence. Here, Solovyov is following a well-walked path by Descartes. Like Descartes, Solovyov questioned the sufficiency of cognitive consciousness as a reliable basis for objectivity. However, he diverged sharply by rejecting the Cartesian *cogito*—"I think, therefore I am"—as a purely subjective affirmation rather than an objective claim. Solovyov likewise critiqued the Kantian transcendental *I*, asserting that it could not serve as the foundational stage of genuine cognition. However, his criticisms rang hollow for even those who couldn't elaborate on who the seat of cognition is (ibid).

What Solovyov does contribute, however, is an insight into the self-referential nature of cognition and its role in affirming an objective moral order.

He argues that "brought to reflexive awareness, the human being's cognitive aspiration and assent to superior values themselves comprise higher-order values which as such intimate the…intrinsic worth of the entire moral order in which they are embedded" (Swiderski 1999, 206). Thus, while he stressed the mystical intuition and experience in his earlier work, he is now concerned with intellectual experiences. This in tandem with the other two can help us achieve universality of reason, and therefore truth.

The ideal of perfection continues to feature prominently, now framed as a developmental progression from lower to higher stages of moral life. This moral ascent begins with the sensual sphere and advances through increasingly refined moral relations. Here we also see a transition from shame to conscience (Solovyov 1996 [1897], 159). There is further development of self-determination which eventually culminates in a self-transcending spiritual self based on the idea of the divine, presenting an order of objective moral Good. Swiderski highlights the parallels of this justification of Good to Solovyov's theoretical philosophy, where the psychological/empirical self moves to the rational self and finally the philosophical self, thereby leading to the truth (Swiderski 1999, 208). In both these cases, the concern is not with an external observer but with the experience of value. Importantly, this progression is not passive; it requires the active participation of the subject in seeking higher stages of both moral and epistemic awareness. As Solovyov writes:

> In order for the idea of the good, in the form of duty, to acquire the force of a sufficient reason or for a motive for action, two factors have to come together: a clarity and adequate fullness of this idea in consciousness and a sufficient moral sensitivity on the part of the subject.
>
> *(Solovyov as quoted in Swiderski 1999, n.a)*

The subject for Solovyov is the human being not as a mortal but as a "form of an infinite content" (Solovyov 1996 [1897], 282). This infinity for him is not bound in its content to ascertain the truth and is within the reach of universal reason. Consequently, the moral order he envisions extends beyond the individual towards a supra-individual structure—a hierarchical movement from the self, to the family, to the community, and ultimately to the universal Church. In this schema, the individual is subordinate to the social whole. Yet, this subordination is not authoritarian but rooted in the moral foundations of society. As Golubev notes, "the dialectic of the relationship between individual and society" in Solovyov's thought is inseparable from his conception of the religious order (Golubev 1978, 51).

Solovyov has often been criticized for allowing religious preoccupations to shape his philosophical conclusions. Yet, his project cannot be reduced to simple religious dogmatism. While theological themes are undeniably central, his philosophy is not merely a religious synthesis but rather an integration of moral philosophy, theoretical epistemology, and metaphysics. In fact, his work challenges metaphysical absolutism and pushes against dogmatic thinking. Despite the explicitly religious language in his writings, many scholars have interpreted and adapted Solovyov's ideas in a secular framework. His intellectual project, ultimately, was not to defend orthodoxy but to overcome the limitations of abstract thinking by constructing a unified philosophical vision that accommodates diverse domains of knowledge.

Conclusion

This chapter has sought to illuminate the complexity and, at times, the inner tensions of Solovyov's philosophical project, especially in the interplay between his moral doctrine and theoretical philosophy. Solovyov's effort to ground moral meaning in a universal Good led him to reject various one-sided positions: the abstract subjectivism of Kant and Tolstoy, the aestheticism of Nietzsche, and the reductionism of positivism. Instead, he proposed that life's meaning lies in its service to the Good, which cannot be reduced to any single domain but must emerge from the synthesis of theological, theoretical, philosophical, and moral spheres.

A central claim of this chapter has been that Solovyov's moral and epistemic spheres are not separable domains, but interdependent dimensions of human experience. His rejection of religious dogmatism does not diminish the role of spiritual intuition; instead, he insists that religious truth must be brought into "the form of a free, intellectual thought" (Solovyov, quoted in Motroshilova 2021, 177). This effort to intellectualize mystical experience reflects his broader philosophical goal: to demonstrate that the pursuit of the Good is as much an epistemological undertaking as it is a spiritual one. In this light, Solovyov's concept of moral experience, grounded in shame, compassion, and reverence, functions as both a mode of knowing and a form of becoming. It is through these morally charged experiences that we encounter not just ethical imperatives, but epistemic insight into the nature of the human and the divine.

Though the chapter has largely focused on Solovyov's theoretical and moral philosophy, it is worth briefly addressing the political dimension of his thought, as it further illuminates the tensions within his vision. Solovyov's political philosophy emerged from his vision of Divine Sophia and his belief in a harmonious, theocratic order. Like other nineteenth-century Russian thinkers, he responded to the legacy of the Church's subordination to the state, imagining instead a "free theocracy" (Zwahlen 2020). This "Christian politics" rests on the idea that conflict is not essential to human society but a symptom of its moral and spiritual fragmentation. As noted by contemporary scholars, Solovyov envisioned an ideal Christian state—one that combines moral authority with political necessity, led by a prophetic intelligentsia, a spiritual monarch (the Tsar), and a universal church (Zweerde 2021). While Solovyov never held political power, his utopian vision shares with revolutionary thinkers like Lenin an anti-political stance: a belief that philosophy is a means of transforming the world, and that true harmony is ultimately achievable through the alignment of metaphysical and ethical life (ibid).

While the political dimensions of his thought, including his at times sympathetic stance toward autocratic ideals, remain a significant and contested aspect of his legacy, they fall outside the scope of this chapter. Nevertheless, they point to a broader question that haunts his work: how metaphysical and moral visions of unity translate into concrete historical or social forms. Ultimately, Solovyov's work offers neither a final doctrine nor a coherent political blueprint. What it provides instead is a philosophical orientation: a conviction that knowledge, morality, and spiritual life are not separate paths but mutually illuminating dimensions of a single human task. His attempt to integrate them, however fraught, remains an invitation to consider how truth and the Good might be approached not through abstraction, but through a life lived towards synthesis.

References

Benedict, Ruth. 1946. *The Chrysanthemum and the Sword: Patterns of Japanese Culture*. Boston: Houghton Mifflin.

Creighton, Millie R. 1990. 'Revisiting Shame and Guilt Cultures: A Forty-Year Pilgrimage'. *Ethos* 18(3): 279–307.

Golubev, A. N. 1978. 'The Concept of the Individual in the Ethics of Vladimir Solovyov'. *Soviet Studies in Philosophy* 17(3): 44–65.

Gubman, Boris L. (Winter 1993). 'The Horizons of the Organic Vision of the Universe and Humanity: Vladimir Solovyev.'. *Process Studies* 22, no. 4: 211–214. Republished at Religion Online (https://www.religion-online.org/article/the-horizons-of-the-organic-vision-of-the-universe-and-humanity-vladimir-solovyev/)

Kant, Immanuel. 1956 (1778). Critique of Practical Reason. Translated by Lewis White Beck. Indianapolis: Bobbs-Merrill.

Kline, George L. 1974. 'Hegel and Solovyov'. In Joseph J. O'Malley, Keith W. Algozin, and Frederick G. Weiss (eds.): *Hegel and the History of Philosophy*. Dordrecht: Springer, pp. 159–170.

Kojève, Alexandre. 2018. *The Religious Metaphysics of Vladimir Solovyov*. Translated by Ilya Merlin and Mikhail Pozdniakov. New York: Springer.

Motroshilova, Nelly. 2021. 'Vladimir Solovyov: Philosophy as Systemic Unity'. In Marina Bykova, Michael Forster, and Lina Steiner (eds.): *The Palgrave Handbook of Russian Thought*. London: Palgrave Macmillan, pp. 159–178.

Navickas, Joseph. 1966. 'Hegel and the Doctrine of Historicity of Vladimir Solovyov'. In Frederick J. Adelmann (ed.): *The Quest for the Absolute*. The Hague: M. Nijhoff, pp. 135–154.

Nemeth, Thomas. (ed.). 2015. *Vladimir Solov'ëv's Justification of the Moral Good: Moral Philosophy*. Berlin: Springer.

Nemeth, Thomas. 2019. *The Later Solov'ëv*. Berlin: Springer.
Obolevitch, T.. 2020. 'The significance of faith in the concept of integral knowledge of Vladimir Solovyov'. *Vestnik of Saint Petersburg University. Philosophy and Conflict Studies*. 36(3): 460–472 https://doi.org/10.21638/spbu17.2020.304
Shein, Louis. 1970. 'V.S. Solov'ev's Epistemology: A Re-examination'. *Canadian Slavic Studies* 4(1): 1–16.
Simons, Andrew. 1999. 'In the Name of the Spirits: A Reading of Solov'ëv's "Justification of the Good"'. *Studies in East European Thought* 51(3): 177–198.
Sládek, Karel. 2010. 'The View of Creation through the Eyes of Vladimir Solovyov and Nikolai Lossky'. *European Journal of Science and Theology* 6(2): 13–19.
Solovyov, Vladimir S. 1990. *War, Progress, and the End of History: Three Conversations*. Hudson: Lindisfarne Press.
Solovyov, Vladimir. 1996 (1897). *The Justification of the Moral Good: Moral Philosophy*. Translated and edited by Thomas Nemeth. Lewiston, NY: Edwin Mellen Press, p. li.
Smerdov, Igor. 2002. *The Philosophical Narrative of Vladimir Solovyov: An Application of Narrative Analysis to Russian Classical Philosophy: A Case-Study of The Crisis of Western Philosophy and Other Works by Vladimir Solovyov*. PhD diss., Katholieke Universiteit Nijmegen.
Smith, Oliver. 2010. *Vladimir Soloviev and the Spiritualization of Matter*. Boston: Academic Studies Press.
Sutton, Jonathan. 1988. *The Religious Philosophy of Vladimir Solovyov: Towards a Reassessment*, Berlin: Springer.
Swiderski, Edward. 1999. 'Vladimir Solov'ëv's "Virtue Epistemology"'. *Studies in East European Thought* 51(3): 199–218.
Zenkovsky, Vasily Vasilyevich. 2003a (1953). *A History of Russian Philosophy*. Vol. 1. Oxfordshire: Taylor & Francis.
Zenkovsky, Vasily Vasilyevich. 2003b (1953). *A History of Russian Philosophy*. Vol. 2. Oxfordshire: Taylor & Francis.
Zwahlen, Regula M. 2020. 'Sergii Bulgakov's Reinvention of Theocracy for a Democratic Age'. *Journal of Orthodox Christian Studies* 3(2): 175–194.
Zweerde, E. van der. 2021. 'Russian Political Philosophy: Between Autocracy and Revolution'. In Marina F. Bykova, Michael N. Forster, and Lina Steiner (eds.): *The Palgrave Handbook of Russian Thought*. London: Palgrave Macmillan, pp. 73–93.

7

THE PHILOSOPHICAL AND SOCIOLOGICAL VIEWS OF N. I. KAREYEV IN THE CONTEXT OF MODERN COGNITIVE MANAGEMENT

Jacopo Agostini

Biography and life

Nikolai Ivanovich Kareev was born on November 24th, 1850 in Moscow to parents belonging to the aristocracy. His father, Ivan Vasilyevich, began his career in the army; however, after being wounded during the Crimean War, he was forced to switch to the civilian sector and later served as governor of several cities in the Smolensk province (Kareev N. I., 1990).

His parents took care of their son with a thorough education in reading, writing, mathematics, French, and geography. Young Nikolai continued his schooling in one of Moscow's gymnasiums and immediately distinguished himself with his talent. In 1869, he graduated from the fifth Moscow Gymnasium and entered the University (Perevedentsev E., 2016; Rushist, n.d.; Skvortsova E. C., n.d.; Tsygankov, 2008). In 1873 he finished his studies at the Department of History and Philology; initially, he chose the Slavic-Russian department and Professor F. I. Buslaev as his academic advisor, but under the influence of the seminars of such distinguished scholars as V. I. Gerje and M. Kutorg and the lectures of his father Sergei Solovyov, he decided to switch to the History department. As early as 1868, the 18-year-old Kareev published his first printed work "Phonetic and Graphic System of the Ancient Hellenic Language" (Фонетическая и графическая система древнего эллинского языка) (Kareev, N. I., 1868; Tsygankov D. A., 2008; Kulalaeva Yu. V., 2020). During this period, Kareev became particularly fascinated by the French Revolution and became interested in the condition of the French peasants. The young historian began collecting material on this subject, which would later remain one of the central themes of his scientific research. This early work of his also won him great praise in France

DOI: 10.4324/9781003541004-8

and earned him a business trip abroad, which he used for the writing of his dissertation "The Peasants and the Peasant Question in France in the Last Quarter of the 18th Century" (Крестьяне и крестьянский вопрос во Франции в последней четверти XVIII века) discussed by the author in 1879 (Myagkov G. P., 2021; Persona, n.d.). The material for his thesis is collected in the National Library and the National Archives of France (Swift T., 2016; Rushist, n.d.).

From 1878 to 1879, Kareev was a guest lecturer at the Department of History and Philology at Moscow University, where he taught a course on the history of the 19th century. In the autumn of 1879, he moved to Poland, which was at that time part of the Russian Empire, and until the end of 1884, he was appointed lecturer extraordinaire at the University of Warsaw. In Poland, Kareev received a new foreign assignment: to write a doctoral thesis. Showing a growing inclination towards sociological research, Kareev titled his thesis "Main Questions of the Philosophy of History" (Основные вопросы философии истории). This work provoked great controversy, to which Kareev responded with a book entitled—"To my critics" (Моим критикам) (Marchenkov, 2015; Perevedentsev E., 2016; Swift T., 2016).

The following year, in 1885, he went to live in St. Petersburg and began teaching first at the Aleksandrovsky lycée, then at St. Petersburg University and from 1896 at the Bestuzhev Courses. In 1890, Kareev became editor of the "Historical Review" (Исторического обозрения) and president of the Historical Society of St. Petersburg University, a position he held until 1917, the same year his book "The Essence of Historical Progress and the Role of the Individual in History" was published. In 1897, he released the first and most comprehensive history of Western sociology at that time, titled "Introduction to the Study of Sociology" (Skvortsova E. C., n.d.; Perevedentsev E., 2016). Kareev then led the course "History of Western Europe in the Modern Era" (История Западной Европы в новое время, Volumes 1–7, 1892–1917), in which not only the cultural and political history of Western Europe in the modern era was studied, but also its socio-economic processes. In 1896, he began teaching history to headmasters and teachers, and in 1897, he took an active part in the Russian Writers Mutual Aid Society (Persona, n.d.).

After the student revolts in 1899 Kareev asked to resign from his professorship at the University of St. Petersburg (thus also leaving the committee of the Society for Needy Students) (Swift T., 2016; Kareev, N. I., n.d.; Skvortsova E. C., n.d.), and the government suspended him from the Bestuzhev Courses for "political unreliability" (Podvoisky D. G., n.d.). He nevertheless retained his position at the Alexander Lyceum and, in the same year, became vice-president of the International Institute of Sociology. Kareev was influenced by the radicalism of Russian thinkers such as Aleksandr Herzen, Dimitrii

Pisarev, Pyotr Lavrov, and N. K. Mikhailovsky, as well as the positivism of Auguste Comte, Herbert Spencer, and John Stuart Mill (Marchenkov, V. 2015; Perevedentsev E., 2016; Podvoisky D. G., n.d.). In 1902, he became a lecturer in the economics department of the St. Petersburg Polytechnic Institute.

Kareev was an appointed chairman of the "Academic Committee" for the Union of Workers of Higher Education, took part in the Literary Fund Committee (of which he became chairman in 1909), and as president of the Department for the Promotion of Self-Education. In 1904, he joined the St. Petersburg Duma (Skvortsova E. C., n.d.) and, for a time became editor of the Historical Department of the Encyclopaedic Dictionary of Brockhaus and Efron (Podvoisky D. G., n.d.; Swift T., 2016).

On January 8, 1905, a day before Gaponov's planned demonstration in the capital, together with a delegation of 10 other members (Maxim Gorky, A. V. Peshekhonov, N. F. Annensky, I. V. Gessen, V. A. Myakotin, V. I. Semevsky, K. K. Arseniev, E. I. Kedrin, N. I. Kareev, and a Haporite worker D. Kuzin), Kareev asks Interior Minister Pyotr Dmitrievich Svyatopolk-Mirsky to cancel certain military measures. The request was refused, and the delegation turned to the Prime Minister of the Russian Empire, Sergei Witte, in the hope of reaching the tsar so that the latter would appear before the workers and accept Gapon's petition. This time, too, the request was rejected. After Bloody Sunday, Kareev was arrested and detained in the Petropavlovsky fortress for 11 days (Swift T., 2016; Rostovtsev, E. A., and Sidorchuk, I. V. n.d.; Rushist, n.d.).

With the onset of the 1905–1907 revolution Kareev, who had long established himself as a liberal, joined the intellectual-constitutionalists and supporters of social reforms (Swift T., 2016) and shares some positivist-evolutionist positions with them (Perevedentsev E., 2016). During the first Russian revolution, Nikolai Ivanovich Kareyev joined the Cadet Party (the party of constitutional democrats), but did not take an active part in its activities, considering himself more capable in scientific work than in politics (Perevedentsev E., 2016; Rostovtsev E. A., and Sidorchuk, I. V., n.d.). This allowed him to join the First State Duma as a deputy, a member of the Kadet faction (Podvoisky D. G., n.d.). However, he soon withdrew from these posts, as he realised that he "was not born for a political career". In 1906, Kareev returned to the University of St Petersburg and devoted himself to scientific work once again.

In 1910, he became a corresponding member of the St. Petersburg Academy of Sciences and continued to publish material on the history of the Parisian revolutionary sections (Unpublished documents on the history of the Parisian sections of 1790–1795, St. Petersburg, 1914; Paris sections during the French Revolution (1790–1795), St. Petersburg, 1911; Political speeches of the Paris sections during the Great Revolution, "Russian wealth," 1912, No 11, etc.) (Certprof, n.d.). In July and August 1914, the scholar was imprisoned in Germany for five weeks.

Kareev's attitude towards the events of 1917 is contradictory. The Russian liberals of the early 20th century, and in particular many Kadets, were largely left-wing and easily collaborated with socialists and radicals during the Duma period. In the First and Second Dumas, Kadets often supported socialist plans for the communitization of the land and bitterly opposed Stolypin's right-wing party. Like many other Kadets, Kareev did not change his liberal ideas, not even in the face of the anarchy that began in Russia after the February 1917 Revolution (Rushist, n.d.). He has always detested political student strikes, cancellations of classes, and countless revolutionary anniversaries. Kareev does not blame the revolution but "the supposedly eternal Russian idleness and the abundance of religious festivals in slave Russia that always prevented the accumulation of cultural and material values." And now all this is automatically transferred to the "new Russia" (Swift T., 2016).

After October 1917, Kareev, unlike many other prominent Russian scientists, did not emigrate abroad but remained in the Soviet state. In 1918, he was arrested again with his entire family in Zaitsevo and remained under house arrest for five days (Swift T., 2016). During the Soviet period, Kareev continued his scientific work, although the new regime increasingly hindered him over the years, once even depriving him of the opportunity to conduct a conference. In 1923, the government decided to stop republishing the scientist's work. In 1928, N. I. Kareev's son Konstantin was arrested and then deported from Leningrad, and the situation worsened further on the eve of Stalin's "great turn" of 1929–1932 (Skvortsova E. C., n.d.).

In 1929, Kareev was appointed an honorary member of the USSR Academy of Sciences (Kareev N. I., n.d.; Perevedentsev E., 2016), although a year later on October 18, 1930 he was subjected to implausible "criticism" at a meeting of the methodological section of the "Society of Marxist Historians" (Общества историков-марксистов) (Swift T., 2016).

He died on February 18, 1931 in Leningrad. He is buried in the cemetery in Smolensk.

His studies and thoughts

Nikolai Ivanovich Kareev is a typical exponent of progressive Russian intellectuality, a generation influenced by the ideas of populist socialism, generally oriented in an anti-bourgeois and anti-capitalist sense, inflamed by the great hopes for renewal aroused by Tsar Alexander II's reforms, but at the same time concerned about the human and social costs that economic development would impose on the rural population; an environment in which overcoming the profound backwardness and misery of the peasant masses was considered the most pressing and significant problem, the ground on which to measure the validity of any reformist and revolutionary political project (Masoero A., 1989).

Kareev deepens the theory of personality, advances the concept of socio-logical education, and revises some problems inherent to the methodology of the social sciences, wanting to overcome some concepts of modern social theories as they are considered by him as "one-sided" (Perevedentsev E., 2016; Sinyutin M. V., 2000; Soboleva N. A., 2013). He introduces an episte-mological view of the theoretical and methodological issues of historical sci-ence that, in his view, would serve as a basis for a generalized analysis of the problem. His studies partly echo the works of his mentor Vladimir Guerrier, a Russian historian and professor of history at Moscow State University.

Kareev challenges Comte's linking of "concrete" history with sociology, moving directly from biology to individual (and not collective, as the Russian scholar suggests) psychology. According to Kareev, the general theory of his-tory is divided into historical epistemology, or historian theory (the theory of historical knowledge), and sociology, which includes social statics and social dynamics (Sinyutin M. V., 2000). The latter includes social morphology, the study of the dynamics through which social phenomena are distributed territorially, and historiology, which deals with the mechanisms of societal development. Sociology and history are disciplines that complement each other but differ in their objects of study and methodology (Certprof, n.d.). Sociology studies society as an object, while history studies it as a process, although both do so in an abstract way. The theoretical basis of Kareev's synthetic constructions is an understanding of the tasks of the philosophy of history, in which he distinguishes historiology (theory of the historical pro-cess—identification of its driving forces, factors, etc.), historiosophy (search for the meaning of history, evaluation of historical events, definition of the purpose of history), and historica (theory of historical knowledge—cogni-tion of history). Together with the methodology of history, which develops questions of historical construction and source criticism, the philosophy of history develops the historian's scientific instrumentarium (Perevedentsev E., 2016; Rostovtsev E. A. and Sidorchuk, I. V., n.d.; Sinyutin M. V., 2000).

Kareev also disagrees with Auguste Comte's "System of Positive Politics" (Malinov A. V. and Dolgova E. A., 2020; Sinyutin M. V., 2000), accord-ing to which the "historical process" is seen as a natural phenomenon and rejects his "three-stage law." Unlike Comte, who sees no distinction between progress and evolution, the Russian author finds in the former a subjective ethics, and in the latter an objective process, differentiating method and theory (Karaseva, 2014; Certprof, n.d.). However, evolution does not always mean progress. Evolution is "a gradual and regular development," and its internal laws derive from and arise out of the comparison and analysis of historical facts.

> Kareev wants to overcome conceptions that deny the laws of the historical process and reduce everything exclusively to them, and likewise rejects theories that overestimate the role of historical heroes and those that assign a decisive role to the masses.
>
> *(Certprof, n.d.; Soboleva N. A., 2013; Kozlova L. A., 2021)*

The main problem for the scholar is the relationship between the individual and the historical process in terms of:

1. Clarification of the content of the historical process
2. Revelation of the role of the individual as the engine of progress
3. Definition of the essence of historical progress

The personality of the individual and society continually influence each other. Kareev focuses on the role of the individual towards the latter in two respects: the representation of the actions of individuals in pragmatic history and in cultural history, on an imaginary ladder where individuals are placed according to the "weight" they have in history. In the lowest rung, we find people who are not independently guided and commanded by the will of others; in the highest rung instead "people who independently conceive of cumulative action and realise it only with the help of extraneous forces" (Certprof, n.d.; Kareev, 1915; Kozlova L. A., 2021). Kareev believes that progress is complex and, above all subjective, covering all aspects of society and the most important areas of human life (Emmons T., 2017). He explains that progress is composed of five subcategories that influence each other:

1) Mental progress
2) Moral progress
3) Political progress
4) Legal progress
5) Economic progress

Central to progress and social organization are personalities, collective psychology (where social phenomena are interpreted as spiritual interactions), and human ideals, and the movement of society is measured on an axiological axis. The formula for progress that Kareev suggests contains three main elements:

1) The ideal, conceptualized as an individual who achieves full personal development through the interplay of individual autonomy and social cohesion.

2) The means to achieve the ideal, i.e. namely the transformation of culture, social practices, and organizational structures through critical discourse, challenging the irrational evolution of the super-organic environment that often contradicts both nature and human forces.
3) The manifestation of the law of progress, which consists in the individual's self-emancipation, where the individual gains agency over the supra-organic environment (Certprof, n.d.).

His idea of development and progress, however, does not lead him to concrete conclusions, and everything is reduced to a subjective, abstract and ill-established formula. Plekhanov criticises Kareev's approach by saying that "despite his tendency towards 'synthesis', Nikolai remains a dualist of the purest water. He has economy here, psychology there; in one pocket the soul, in the other the body. There is an interaction between these substances, but each of them leads its own independent existence, whose origin is covered by the darkness of obscurity" (Certprof, n.d.).

For Kareev, society is a complex environment (supra-organic environment) within which social interactions and practices are born and formed, and the determining factor for its development is spiritual culture. The author takes an eclectic approach and a pluralistic sociological method (Malinov A.V. and Dolgova E.A., 2020), and wants to synthesise idealism and materialism into a single theory, which for the Russian author is largely feasible in a society where the individual is both body and spirit. Revealing the importance of private humanities (social sciences) for sociology, Kareev wrote: "Sociology inherited the idea of society from statescience. Sociology has inherited the notion of society as a society bounded in space. A society bounded externally and organised internally, with a history over time" (Malinov A.V. and Dolgova E.A., 2020).

Kareev divides society into cultural groups and social organizations. The former are concerned with the ideas, interactions, aspirations and emotions of members of society (individual psychological approach), which are formed and consolidated through practices of education, imitation and habit. Social organizations, on the other hand, are the fruit and study of collective psychology and are indicators of personal freedom. In society, psychological relationships are channelled and take shape in social institutions and forms (Certprof, n.d.). Kareev argues that social organization is the totality of the legal, economic, and political environment, at the basis of which lies the individual (Malinov A.V. and Dolgova E.A., 2020; Kareev, 1897). Besides, in every society there is a spiritual system, a variety of forms. If one studies its place in society and economic life, one speaks of a political and economic system. If one deals with relations between private individuals under state authority, one speaks of a legal system. Therefore, one could say, Kareev specified, that state, law, and economic science, when positively grounded, only produce material for sociology, but not everything they produce is valuable for sociology, and sociology itself must pose many questions that are broader and more comprehensive than those posed by these sciences (Malinov A.V. and Dolgova E.A., 2020).

As a student, Kareev collaborated with various journals such as the Voronezh "Филогические записки" and "Знание." He devoted his early writings to the history of the French peasantry, which in 1881 took shape in his dissertation "Очерк истории франц. крестьянства." Between 1911 and 1915, he focused his studies on the history of the revolutions in Paris and, ten years later, published the three-volume work "Историки французской революции." The first historiographical work of value on the Great French Revolution for both Russian and foreign academics (Masoero A., 1989). His work on the peasant question was praised and described as very "conscientious" by Karl Marx and Friedrich Engels (Kareev N. I., n.d.; Kulalaeva Yu. V., 2020). Peter Kropotkin, Russian libertarian, philosopher, and anarchist militant, refers to Kareev as one of the few scholars who managed to understand the French Revolution because he had studied "the movements that preceded it" (Kropotkin, 1902).

The study of the French Revolution was not allowed in Russia until the time of Alexander II's reforms. In 1868, Vladimir Guerrier, a professor at Moscow University, announced a seminar dedicated to the French Revolution (Voir T. I. 1989). This date is considered the starting point for studies on the French Revolution in Russia. Over the next thirty years, Russian historians published works that held their own against the best publications of French historiography, whose tradition was much older. In fact, Russian historiography had not only assimilated the results of French research but had become an integral part of European historiography (Tchoudinov A., 2014). Kareev himself recalls that among non-French scholars, no one in the last 30 or 35 years has contributed to the study of the French Revolution and the Old Regime equal to that of Russian historians (Kareev N. I., 1911: 318). He who began his conscious life in the 1870s could not help but ponder when and how the long Western European revolution, in its irresistible flow, would take over Russia (Kareev N. I., 1990: 289). He himself explained in the preface to the French edition of his book that he had approached the subject because he was struck by the parallel between the end of serfdom in Russia and the feudal abolition decrees of 1789. Kareev writes, in essence, a social history of the Revolution from the point of view of the rural plebs and describes the fundamental peasant aspirations that took on the social problem (Masoero A., 1989).

Kareev is also the first major exponent of a particular line of social history research devoted to the state of the countryside and the peasant movement before and during the Revolution (Masoero A., 1989). In writing his work, he made use of press materials, archival material from the Paris Commune

(Rostovtsev E. A. and Sidorchuk I. V., n.d.) and even the electoral mandates of 1789, demonstrating that the condition of the peasantry was burdened by continuous and intense feudal oppression, which he named 'feudal reaction'. With his work, he contradicted Alexis de Tocqueville: the latter claimed that the peasants lived in a society without feudal relations with the owners of their land (Kareev N. I., n.d.). Kareev's target was rather the risk, which he saw as inherent in the Tocquevillian conception of the Revolution as a legal recognition of an already existing social structure, of underestimating the actual seriousness of the agrarian problem at the end of the century and the acuteness of the social contrasts in the rural world, and thus of downplaying the importance of the abolition of feudalism as a fundamental political node in the revolutionary process that began with '89. Kareev accurately describes the French pre- and post-revolution split: "the semi-medieval peasantry versus the rural bourgeoisie and proletariat" (Certprof, n.d.; Lenin V. I., 1960: 231). In his conclusions, also based on detailed and meticulous research in the cohiers de doléances he finds: the backwardness of cultivation methods, the extreme inequality, variety and fragmentation in the distribution of land, sharecropping as the prevailing form of peasant agriculture, the progressive differentiation of the peasant class between a stratum of labourers and one of well-to-do cultivators, in parallel with the formation of a rural bourgeoisie of peasant origin. The fundamental preconditions for the revolutionary outbreak were thus the failure to resolve the agrarian question together with the worsening of the peasant condition during the second half of the 18th century. The peasant movement, although differentiated internally, continued to follow its own logic and dynamics, acting in a dialectical and conflictual relationship with the Parisian political centre (Masoero A., 1989).

Kareev considered himself a "semi-positivist" and an ethical individualist, like Lavrov, although more detached from the works of Hegel or Karl Marx and more Kantian than the latter. He argued for the autonomy of the individual against the three anti-individualist currents of thought:

1) David Hume's idea where the self is a mere fiction, a succession of impressions and suppositions.
2) Hegel's idea where the individual is brought back to the concept of the Zeitgeist or Volksgeist.
3) Marx's idea where the subject is a product in relation to socio-economic dynamics.

Kareev is convinced that everyone's happiness, dignity, worth, and spiritual growth are related to his or her being free on the socio-political level (Kareev N. I., 1895). He rejects all utilitarian thinking about the individual that transforms and reduces him into an object and disregards his absolute value as an individual as such. It is therefore necessary to consider both, as Lavrov emphasises in his studies, his natural rights and his inherent potential for intellectual and moral development and growth. To this end, he openly condemns political assassination, capital punishment, and euthanasia. Also close to this thought are Immanuel Kant, and Lev Tolstoy, whose philosophy of history, however, has been criticised by Kareev (Marchenkov V., 2015). As for the relationship with neo-Kantianism, he suggests that sociology as an "abstract general science about the nature, genesis and laws governing social phenomena" is a "nomological" (legislative) science, whereas history and the philosophy of history are a "phenomenological" science, examining specific combinations and mutual connections of past events. Sociology eliminates any element of individuality and causality from historical facts and determines the meaning of social laws, the result of the will, order, and regularity of thought of individuals. Kareev is convinced that his ideas preceded those of the scholars Simmel, Rickert, and Windelband, who divided science into "nomothetic", which establishes laws, and ideographic, which concerns separate and individual objects (Certprof, n.d.; Karaseva, 2014; Sinyutin M. V., 2000). "Thus, for Kareev, there is a separation of history from sociology, of phenomenon from essence, the concrete is opposed to the abstract, the actual course of history is opposed to some ideal formulae" (Certprof, n.d.). Kareev thinks that social phenomena have a psychic basis and arise as a result of the spiritual and emotional-volitional interaction of individuals. The scholar therefore focuses on the relationship between the individual as the "source" of creativity and cultural innovation and the social environment, which limits and regulates human actions. He argues that all cultural phenomena—language, literature, art, etc. (i.e. culture in the narrow sense of "spiritual life" or "folk psychology") belong not to sociology, but to collective psychology. Spiritual culture is also capable of influencing social life, and from this it can certainly be of interest to sociologists. According to him, the social role of spiritual culture is that the system either finds in it a strengthening support or it can only be expected to have a debilitating effect on the mind. The social function of culture is to bring people together based on language and shared beliefs, not just close political or economic interests. The study of culture can reveal the social role of ideas and values (Malinov A. V. and Dolgova E. A., 2020). His general antimetaphysical positivist attitude is combined with the idea that it is impossible to eliminate the "subjective element" (the scientist's worldview, moral judgements, etc.) from the research practice of the social sciences (Podvoisky D. G., n.d.). The scholar argues that "reason, thought, ideas do not belong to the world as a whole, but to the world within the boundaries of human knowledge" (Certprof, n.d.), so the meaning that history has is not absolute but subjective for each individual. And Kareev is one of the last scholars to combine the subjective method with theoretical development in sociology (Certprof, n.d.). He makes a distinction between casual and regular subjectivism. The former concerns the personal and intrinsic characteristics of the scholar, such as his emotions, interests and mentality, while the latter is linked to his social position, i.e. his membership of a certain group, political class, etc. According to Kareev, one must eliminate both casual subjectivism and the regular, as elements that influence the course of research. The scientist must "rise" above all religious, social, economic, and class forms and interests, but never alienate the subjectivism contained within the process of cognition. The social sciences are not the realm of subjectivity, for if the starting point of the investigation is subjective, it does not mean that the results obtained are also subjective. Even if the sociologist starts from individual and subjective premises, as the bearer of "legitimate subjectivism", of a certain class and social forces, through the rigorous application of a method, he arrives at objective and scientific conclusions (Certprof, n.d.). Kareev, partly echoing Aleksandr Herzen's "philosophy of chance", states that "history is not a straight line, it is not a regular pattern drawn on a mathematical plane, but a living fabric of irregular and sinuous lines, which intertwine in the most varied and unexpected ways," and only makes sense from the subjective moral aspect, where human progress has its own meaning only if it is linked to human destiny (Kareev N. I., 1883: 153; Certprof, n.d.). Comparative and historical study is useful in anticipation of sociological thinking, wherein events and principles are evaluated from the point of view of a specific ideal (Certprof, n.d.). He remains a critic of Marxist social theory and, while recognising its partial correctness, emphasises the limitations of any monistic explanatory model of social life, deeming their claims to intellectual exclusivity unfounded and deeming them "underdeveloped" and "dogmatic." Remaining in Soviet Russia after 1917, Kareev cultivated the idea of a theoretical synthesis between Marxist economism and the psychologism of the "subjective school" (Podvoisky D. G., n.d.). He, together with some liberal populists, wrote a series of articles against "pure" Marxism and economic materialism published under the name "Old and new studies on economic materialism" (1896) (Certprof, n.d.), later criticised and ridiculed by Plekhanov and Lenin (Lenin V. I., 1960: 394). Kareev was a member, together with I. V. Luchitsky, M. M. Kovalevsky, and P. G. Vinogradov, of the famous "Russian school" ("École russe") of historians and sociologists of his time who also shared an interest in the study of the agrarian question in the French Revolution. The Russian school was highly appreciated by K. Marx and F. Engels, and it was the latter who considered the "école russe" to be characterised by "critical thinking and a disinterested pursuit of pure theory" that "stood infinitely above everything that had been created in this respect in Germany and France by official historical science"

(Podvoisky D. G., n.d.). From the Soviet Union, however, this thought was criticised and judged as a "subjective-psychological approach." He took an active part in the polemics of various schools and trends of social thought in the second half of the 19th and the beginning of the 20th century. At the beginning of the 20th century, he is considered the greatest historiographer of pre-revolutionary Russian sociology (Podvoisky D. G., n.d.). His work was deeply connected with the empirical research of the social aspects, particularly those concerning French history. He made minute observations of the French historical plots: "very valuable results" were achieved by "immense archival work". This empirical basis of the works allowed Kareev to make "broad generalizations", and the French historians followed this closely and underlined more than once the "importance of Russian works", often using the term "Russian school" (Vasiliev Y. A., 2024).

Publications and meetings

Before the Revolution, Nikolai Ivanovich Kareev was famous as the author of exemplary history texts for grammar schools and universities. Kareev's "Handbook of Ancient History" was published no less than nine times, the "Handbook of Medieval History" ten times and the "Handbook of New History" sixteen times, translated into Bulgarian, Polish, and partly into Serbian. Nikolai Kareev in "Истории Западной Европы в Новое время" changed the practice of handing down the names of European monarchs: the Ludovici became Ludwigs, and the Franks became Francises (Ustinov V, 2020).

Kareyev's multi-volume university lectures were published under the title History of Western Europe in Modern Times "История Западной Европы в новое время". In compiling his textbooks, Kareev had a world-historical perspective, highlighting issues of foreign policy, economic or cultural development, i.e. what was most important in the life of one or another nation at a particular time (Skvortsova E. C., n.d.). In total, Kareev wrote more than 400 scientific works. This does not include unpublished archival material, which totals about 12 thousand sheets (Perevedentsev E., 2016).

His stay in Warsaw gave Kareev a long-standing interest in Polish history (Rushist, n.d.). He devoted many of his works, articles, and books to it, some of which were translated into Polish and brought Kareev great popularity both in Russia and abroad. These include "The fall of Poland in the historical literature" (Падение Польши в исторической литерату пе), 1889; "Outline of the History of the Reformation Movement and the Catholic Reaction in Poland" (Очерк истории реформационного движения и католической реакции в Польше), 1886; "Historical Review of the Polish Sejm" (Исторический очерк польского сейма), 1888; "Polish reforms XVIII century" (Польские реформы XVIII в.), 1890; "Causes de la chute de la Pologne," 1893, and others (Swift T, 2016; Person, n.d.).

In his third category of works "Основные вопросы философии истории" (2nd ed., 1887), under the name "Сущность исторического процесса и роль личности в истории" in the third edition (1890), "Философия культурной и социальной истории нового времени" (1893) and "Историко-философск ие и социлогические этюды" 1895, he studies the historical development of sociology in Russia.

During his innumerable trips abroad, Kareev had the opportunity to get to know many important personalities. Kareev had significant academic relations with several Czech and Slovak intellectuals, such as Jaroslav Bidlo, Jaroslav Goll, Josef Pekař, and Ľubomír Niederle (Daniš M., 2020). In France, Kareev engaged with scholars like Fustel de Coulanges and Alphonse Aulard, as well as with Gabriel Monod, the editor-in-chief of *Revue Historique*, for whom Kareev contributed articles. He also interacted with Charles-Victor Langlois and Charles Seignobos, leading figures of the *école méthodique*, and Henri Berr, editor of the journal La synthese historique. Kareev sympathised with Berr's theories, and it was for this reason that he wrote a positive review of the book "La synthese en histoire" (The Synthesis in History) (Berelowitch W., 2008). He was very close to Kovalevskii and knew Rend Worms, Gabriel Tarde, Alfred Espinas, and Lester Ward, but appears to have overlooked the pivotal contributions of Durkheim's foundational theories and the significant insights of Max Weber's sociological work (Worms to Kareev, 1916).

Bibliography

Berelowitch W. 2008. History in Russia comes of age: institution-building, cosmopolitanism, and theoretical debates among historians in late imperial Russia. https://www.thefreelibrary.com/History+in+Russia+comes+of+age%3a +institution-building%2c...-a0251726661 (accessed on 27 September 2022)

Certprof. n.d. https://certprof.ru/en/with-your-own-hands/kareev-n-i-nikolai -ivanovich-kareev-kareev-nikolai-ivanovich/ (accessed on 21 September 2022)

Daniš M. 2020. N.I. Kareev in the Czech and Slovak history and historiography. Uchenye Zapiski Kazanskogo Universiteta. *Seriya Gumanitarnye Nauki*, vol. 162, no. 6, pp. 99–110. https://doi.org/10.26907/2541-7738.2020.6.99-110

Emmons T. 2017. History and politics in Russia before the revolution. *Journal of Modern Russian History and Historiography*, vol. 10, no. 1, pp. 112–124. https://doi.org/10.1163/22102388-01000005

Karaseva T.A. 2014. *N.I. Kareev as a theorist of historical methodology of the XIX century [Н.И. Кареев как теоретик исторической методологии XIX века]. In From Crisis to Modernization: World Experience and Russian Practice of Fundamental and Applied Research [От кризисак модернизации: мировой опыт и российская практика фундаментальных и прикладных научных разработок] (pp. 64–66). Saint Petersburg Institute of Project Management. KultInform Press.*

Kareev N.I. 1868. *Phonetic and graphical system of the ancient Greek language.* Moscow: Typ. T. Risy. (Published in 1869).

Kareev N.I. 1883. Osnovnye voprosy filosofii istorii (Fundamental problems in the philosophy of history). https://archive.org/details/osnovnyevoprosyf121kare/page/n5/mode/2up?ref=ol&view=theater (accessed on 17 September 2022).

Kareev N.I. 1895. Mysli ob osnovakh nravstvennosti (Thoughts on the foundations of morality). https://babel.hathitrust.org/cgi/pt?id=inu.30000000219216&view=1up&seq=5&skin=2021 (accessed on 17 September 2022)

Kareev N.I. 1897. *Introduction to the study of sociology.* St. Petersburg: M. Stasyulevych's printing house. XVI, 418 p.

Kareev N.I. 1911. Последние работы русских ученых о французской революции in Вестник Европы no. 4.

Kareev N. I. 1915. *Historiology.* Petrograd: Printing house of M. M. Stasyulevich

Kareev N.I. 1990. Прожитое и пережитое. Л. https://archive.org/details/1990_20230829 (accessed on 26 July 2024).

Kareev N.I. n.d. *The great soviet encyclopedia*, 3rd edition, 1970–1979. https://encyclopedia2.thefreedictionary.com/Nikolai+Ivanovich+Kareev (accessed on 30 July 2024).

Kozlova L.A. 2021. Переход от истории к социологии в учении Н.И. Кареева и историческая социология [Transition from history to sociology in the teachings of N.I. Kareev and historical sociology]. *Историческая социология* , vol. 10, pp. 1–20. https://doi.org/10.31857/S013216250013810-4

Kropotkin P. 1902. Kropotkin to Nettlau, March 5, 1902: On Individualism and the Anarchist Movement in France. Revoltlib. https://www.revoltlib.com/anarchism/kropotkin-to-nettlau-march-5-1902-france-kropotkin-peter-1902/ (accessed on 12 September 2022).

Kulalaeva Yu. V. 2020. Anniversaries in the World of Science. Nikolay Kareev – Russian historian and sociologist. https://nbmariel.ru/content/yubilyary-v-mire-nauki-nikolay-kareev-rossiyskiy-istorik-i-sociolog (accessed on 30 August 2024)

Lenin V.I. 1902. Lenin collected works Vol-5. https://archive.org/details/in.ernet.dli.2015.97507/mode/2up?q= (accessed on 24 September 2022).

Lenin V.I. 1960. Lenin collected works Vol-1. https://archive.org/details/dli.ernet.506160/mode/2up (accessed on 24 September 2022).

Malinov A.V. and Dolgova E.A. 2020. Sociology as a theoretical science (Based on Nikolay Kareyev's Manuscript "General Methodology of the Humanities"). *Sotsiologicheskiy Zhurnal = Sociological Journal*, vol. 26, no. 4, pp. 116–136. https://doi.org/10.19181/socjour.2020.26.4.7646

Marchenkov V. 2015. KAREEV, NIKOLAI IVANOVICH. encyclopedia. https://www.encyclopedia.com/humanities/encyclopedias-almanacs-transcripts-and-maps/kareev-nikolai-ivanovich-1850-1931 (accessed on 12 September 2022).

Masoero A. 1989. Nikolai Ivanovich Kareev. In Bongiovanni B. and Guerci L. (eds.), *L' albero della Rivoluzione. Le interpretazioni della Rivoluzione francese.* Einaudi, pp. 323–327.

Myagkov G.P. 2021. "The Legacy of N.I. Kareev is Extremely Relevant at the Beginning of the 21st Century." Interview - Conversation with Professor V.P. Zolotarev // Nikolai Ivanovich Kareev: Life Path and Scientific Heritage in the Transdisciplinary Context of Modern Historiography: Collection of Articles and Messages / compiled and edited by G.P. Myagkov. Kazan: Kazan University Publishing House, pp. 347–364. Kareev-conf2020.pdf (kpfu.ru)

Perevedentsev E. 2016. Николай Иванович Кареев. Proza. https://proza.ru/2016/11/20/1763 (accessed on 20 September 2022).

Persona. n.d. https://persona.rin.ru/eng/view/f/0/24224/kareev-nikolai-ivanovich (accessed on 27 September 2022).

Podvoisky D.G. N.d. КАРЕ́ЕВ. Bigenc. https://bigenc.ru/philosophy/text/2046336 (accessed on 15 September 2022).

Rostovtsev E.A. and Sidorchuk I.V. n.d. *Кареев Николай иванович , Биографика СПбГУ* . https://bioslovhist.spbu.ru/person/376-kareev-nikolay-ivanovich.html (accessed on 29 August 2024).

Rushist. n.d. Кареев, Николай Иванович. http://rushist.com/index.php/historians /1548-kareev-nikolaj-ivanovich (accessed on 28 September 2022).

Sinyutin M.V. 2000. On the methodology of N.I. Kareev. In N.I. Kareev (ed.), *Sociology of history*, vol. 2. Saint Petersburg State University, pp. 277–280.

Skvortsova E.C. n.d. АКАДЕМИК НИКОЛАЙ ИВАНОВИЧ КАРЕЕВ И ЕГО УЧЕБНИК ДРЕВНЕЙ ИСТОРИИ. https://www.istmira.com/uchebnik-drevnej -istorii/1980-akademik-nikolaj-ivanovich-kareev-i-ego-uchebnik.html (accessed on 28 September 2022).

Soboleva N.A. 2013. *Личность как «мерило культуры» в рефлексии Н . И. Кареева (1850–1931).* Тверской государственный технический университет.

Swift T. 2016. Николай Иванович Кареев. Proza. https://proza.ru/2016/06/15/480 (accessed on 15 September 2022).

Tchoudinov A. 2014. l'école historique russe et la révolution française: vladimir ger'e et nikolaj kareev à propos d'hippolyte taine et d'alphonse aulard. *Revue Des Études Slaves*, vol. 85, no. 1, pp. 57–66. http://www.jstor.org/stable/24372646

Tsygankov D.A. 2008. *V.I. Guerrier and the Moscow University of his era.* Moscow: State Pedagogical University. 256 c.

Ustinov V. 2020. Why is Henry not Henry and Ludovic not Ludovic? // *Science and Life*, № 2. - C. 96.

Vasiliev Y.A. 2024. *«Russian School» («Ecole russe») as a precedent international recognition in historical science at the turn of the 19th – 20th centuries.* In *Russian science: Past, present, future* (pp. 77–84). Moscow: ISPI FNISC RAS.

Voir T.I. 1989. Vladimir Guerrier et les débuts de l'études, en Russie, de la Révolution française. In *la Révolution française et la Russie.* Moskva: éditions du Progrès, pp. 146–157.

Worms to Kareev, 10 December 1916. Russian State Library (RGB), f. 119 (Kareev), papka 32, ed. khr. 9, ll. 1-1 ob.

8

REVISITING THE "POSITIVE PHILOSOPHY" THROUGH THE LIFE AND WORK OF EUGÈNE DE ROBERTY

The foundational scholar of Franco-Russian sociology in the 19th century

Ahmed Abidur Razzaque Khan and Abdur Razzaque Khan

Introduction

Eugene Valentinovich De Roberty (1843–1915) was a Russian-French sociologist and the leading social thinker of pre-revolutionary Russia. He was one of the first intellectuals to work for the recognition of sociology as a science by formulating it in 1880. As one of the most systematic thinkers and philosophers from the end of the 19th century to the beginning of the 20th century in Russia, his activities and publications make him a significant figure, especially for that period in developing scientific sociological knowledge. Moreover, as one of the leading social thinkers of pre-revolutionary Russia, who addressed social solidarity, cooperation, and altruism, he became a remarkable figure at home and abroad. He is considered one of the fathers of Russian and European sociology.

This fairly well-known neo-positivist scientist carried out most of his activities within St. Petersburg, which allowed him to be not only a member of various associations but also to become a co-founder of the first department of sociology in Russia, which for some time he headed together with another well-known Russian sociologist, M. M. Kovalevsky. However, the irony is that his sociological works were even condemned by the Holy Synod (the governing institution of the Russian Orthodox Church) and were withdrawn from libraries (Efremenko & Evseeva, 2012). Not much appreciated by his own country or society in his lifetime. Unfortunately, his contribution to western and Russian scholarship is still little known in the history of sociology and the present world.

The objective of this chapter is to present an overview of the life and work of De Roberty and his contribution to the Russian sociological tradition.

DOI: 10.4324/9781003541004-9

This chapter aims to shed light on De Roberty's work and life and assess his contribution to his country Russia, the western world, and the field of sociology.

Life and work: an overview

Eugène de Roberty was a distinguished philosopher and sociologist of the late 19th and early 20th centuries. Though this unsung hero of the European intellectual community devoted his whole life to pursuing knowledge, especially establishing sociology as a discipline, he is not acknowledged as one of the founder of the discipline. P. Sorokin is probably the last sociologist who made a sufficiently objective presentation of the work of de Roberty, who is entirely forgotten by Western sociologists. As P. Sorokin (1927, 1938: 305) acknowledges:

> The philosophical and didactic character of his reasoning, as well as a heavy style, undoubtedly explain why his name is much less known than those of Durkheim or Simmel, whose theories de Roberty proposed earlier and, in some ways, with more consequences.

Since the early nineties in Russia, the works of de Roberty have been an integral part of current research on the history of Russian sociology. As a result, de Roberty is considered one of the founders of Russian and European sociology. Apart from this, he was one of the first intellectuals to work for the recognition of sociology as a science in 1880. However, de Roberty, from the start until the end of his intellectual life, was very reluctant about any biological explanation of the social phenomenon (Semlali, 2005).

On December 13, 1843, Eugene Valentiovich de Roberty de Castro de la Cerda was born in the Kazankoe village in the Podolsk administration. His father, Valentin, was descended from two aristocratic families: one Spanish (from Castro de la Cerda) and the other French (from Roberty). Eugene's great-grandfather, Francois de Roberty, emigrated to Russia during the reign of Catherine II. His son Charles took Russian citizenship in 1796 and joined the army. Charles married the daughter of Charles de Castro de la Cerda. Very little is known about Roberty's mother. She was a Tatar from the Simbirsk region. Eugene's father was sick, and his mother took care of him.

He pursued an extensive and rigorous education across some of Europe's most esteemed institutions. He studied at the Moscow Gymnasium, the Alexander Lyceum, Heidelberg, Giessen, and Jena Universities. Born into a noble family, he commenced his studies at the Moscow Gymnasium before being sent, at the age of nine, to the prestigious Imperial Alexander Lyceum in St. Petersburg. His noble lineage granted him admission to the Lyceum at the age of twelve, where he continued his academic journey until the age of nineteen.

During his time at the Alexander Lyceum, de Roberty formed significant intellectual connections, including an acquaintance with the young Count Grigory Nikolaevich Vyrubov in 1857 (Lioubina, 2004: 84–107). Following his foundational education in Russia, he broadened his academic pursuits by studying at renowned universities in Heidelberg, Giessen, and Jena, where he engaged with contemporary European philosophical and sociological thought.

At the end of 1862, de Roberty was admitted to the small university of Heidelberg, where he found 100 Russian students at the university. Accordingly, de Roberty enrolled at the university on May 18, 1863. De Roberty came to Germany to study political science and economics. He found some brilliant teachers at the University of Heidelberg, like R. von Mohi and Bluntschi. He was a law student but had a keen interest in biology. Later, on November 22, 1864, de Roberty left Heidelberg to attend the esteemed University of Jena, where he successfully defended his Ph.D. "Some clarifications on the inner constitution of Grand Novgorod in the Middle Ages" was the title of his doctoral thesis. His diverse educational background contributed to his later work, which blended Russian intellectual traditions with Western European influences. Not only that, he was surrounded by a highly supportive and intellectually productive circle. In the winter of 1864–1865, he travelled to Berlin, where he spent time with his close friend G. Wyroubov. Later, the two collaborated on translating Émile Littré's *Words of Positive Philosophy and Comments on Herzen*, helping to disseminate the influential thinker's ideas to a broader audience.

Émile Littré played a crucial role in the development of early sociology, and in 1872, a group of intellectuals who rallied around his ideas founded the first sociological society. Among its 26 founding members was Eugène de Roberty, whose contributions helped shape the emerging discipline. This initiative arose in the wake of the Franco-Prussian War and the violent suppression of the Paris Commune, reflecting a broader intellectual effort to understand and address societal upheavals.

In 1867, Littré co-founded *La Philosophie Positive*, a bimonthly journal dedicated to advancing the positivist philosophy of Auguste Comte. One of his close collaborators in this endeavour was the young Russian count Grégoire Wyrouboff, who would later become a key figure in positivist intellectual circles. De Roberty, too, became an active and vibrant contributor to the journal, engaging deeply with its intellectual discourse.

Wyrouboff's involvement with Littré intensified after his relocation to Paris in 1864. He played a crucial role in managing *La Philosophie Positive*, shaping its direction, and fostering discussions on positivism (Heilborn, 2009). This network of thinkers—including Littré, Wyrouboff, and de Roberty—created a dynamic intellectual environment that significantly influenced the development of positivist and sociological thought in the late 19th century.

However, due to family responsibilities, he had to temporarily step away from his academic and intellectual pursuits abroad. According to Semliali, in 1866, Eugène de Roberty left Germany and returned to Russia to be with his ailing father in the village of Valentinovka, located in the Government of Tver. His father had a lumber business there and had stayed for years. After that, he settled down in the countryside to lead the life of a rural farmer. He often used to leave his village to go to St. Petersburg. As per the note of M. Kovalevsky (June 1915: 161), Roberty informed his friend G. Wyroubov of his desire to launch a positive review. He explained:

Various material circumstances oblige me to seek a source of income that will depend only on my personal work. This is how I imagined a political, economic, and financial review, review sui generis, where one would print only front-page articles on the issues of the day, appearing weekly, and is the size of a printing press. We only want to address ourselves to Russian intellectuals without distinguishing which party they might belong to. As for politics, we want to find a party, and political intellectuals, and for economic and financial questions, we will try to be the pioneers Della Scienza Nuova, of new science (the name given to sociology long before its foundation by Comte, by the Italian Vico).

Since 1887 he lived and worked abroad, where he published his most significant works on philosophy, sociology, and ethics, all in French. In 1869 he published his first influential book, Politico-Economic Studies, the merit of which was the substantiation of the need for the socialization of political economy. After losing his brother in 1870, Roberty left teaching and began his journalistic career. He continued journalism for three years and was one of the collaborators of VF Korsch, editor-in-chief of Saint Peterburg's News, regulated by the Russian Academy of Science. It was a daily newspaper and the only opposition press that defended liberal ideas against conservative doctrines. However, he could not continue with journalism as DA Tolstoi, the then Minister of Public Education, sent a report to the Emperor about the newspaper and declared de Roberty and the editor-in-chief VF Korsh as "harmful collaborators," As a result, the Ministry of Education took complete control of the Saint Petersburg News on January 1, 1875. It replaced the entire editorial board with a new one.

De Roberty actively worked to popularize the idea of Auguste Comte in Russia. From 1876 to 1878, he carried out his project by actively participating in the life of the Sociological Society and its organ, the Positive Philosophy. In fact, during this period, nine of his articles containing 213 pages were published. The first six articles (1876–1877) dealt with the sociological problem, the place of sociology among the sciences, and its internal division. In 1878, his three articles were published under the title of

"Sociological Notes." However, it is a fact that since the publication of his first work on sociology in 1881, his thought has not been well accepted in Russia; rather, it was more favourably received in France. His "The Past of Philosophy" (vols. 1–2, 1886) was especially banned from public libraries for liberal ideas.

As a man, he was not just an intellectual or thinker. In 1874, at the age of 31, we see he got married to Ekaterina Alexandrovna Glazenap, who was from an aristocratic family. She came either from a family of German Catholic immigrants or from a Polish upper-class family. It reflects the diversity and flexibility of his life and his vision. In 1894, at the age of 51, he was a professor at the New Brussels University and taught there until 1907. Later, he became one of the organizers of the Russian Higher School of Social Sciences, which opened in Paris and attracted the attention of many researchers who would then contribute to the development of sociological science. From 1908 to 1915, de Roberty served as a professor of sociology at the Psychoneurological Institute in St. Petersburg, contributing to the advancement of social science in Russia.

As the neo-positivist leader, he was recognized as one of the founders of European sociology at that time. He had been a member of the International Sociological Institute in Paris since 1893. He was elected as the adviser of the Société de sociologie in 1906. In 1908 he published his Sociology of Action. At the beginning of the same year, he became the chair of sociology at the Psycho-neurological Institute in St. Petersburg, where he worked as a professor until 1915, until his assassination on May 8. However, we cannot call him just an ivory tower thinker or pure academic as he actively participated in Social Movements. In 1914, with Kovalevsky, he published New Ideas in Sociology collection.

Eugène de Roberty's life was marked by remarkable academic achievements and a distinguished career in sociology. By the age of 21, in 1864, he had already completed his doctoral degree, successfully defending his dissertation at the University of Jena. His thesis focused on the socio-political structure of the Novgorod Republic in the Middle Ages, reflecting his deep engagement with historical and sociological analysis.

Tragically, at the age of 72, just as his ideas were gaining increasing recognition across Europe, his life was cut short. On May 8, 1915, he was murdered on his estate by a robber named Dangichev, bringing a sudden and violent end to a life dedicated to intellectual and academic pursuits.

Key though, and his time

What would be the ideal concept of sociology in modern times? How is it different from other academic knowledge and sciences? Those are the key objectives of this Russian sociologist's whole life, thought, and work. The

Russian scholar seconded his argument on sociology by publishing his first work on sociology (1881) in Russian and French. In addition, he defended his position in the international congress of sociology and other forums.

Throughout the 19th century, Auguste Comte's (1798–1857) positive philosophy and his agenda for a new science of human society were intensely debated in intellectual circles of Europe. However, during that time, Russian culture and society were under the strong influence of the Orthodox Church. Therefore, even in the works of liberal representatives of the Westernizer tradition of Russian social thought, the discussion of cohesion issues was less prioritized due to religious inferences. However, a rich tradition of solidarity studies existed until the revolution of 1917, which was based on Marxist ideology. According to the study by Dimitry Efremenko and Yaroslava Evseeva, one driving force revealed in the last third of the 19th century through the influence of Fyodor Dostoevsky's widely read works is the radicalization of Russian traditionalism. Another stream is based on Western Europe's strategic orientation towards values and institutional practices (2012). De Roberti belonged to the second group.

Eugène de Roberty appeared as Russia's first professional sociologist who simultaneously published all of his work in French. Although de Roberty is primarily recognized as a positivist thinker, he strongly criticized purely biological approaches to explaining sociological evolution, emphasizing the role of cognitive reasoning in social development. Pitirim Sorokin mentioned de Roberty as his teacher and recognized that his thought considerably influenced the further development of the studies of social solidarity.

At that time, sociology was not established as a new science or field of study. As we see, sociology was noticeably underdeveloped in comparison to the other positive sciences and several works written after 1870. Comte had analogously conceptualized sociology, and it took several decades to create a new science of "sociology" which led to a small corpus of studies. Littré opined that sociology since Comte—had been endowed with a systematic conception and was founded on the law of history, the direction of progress, the march of civilization, and the aim of humanity (Heilbron, 2009).

During that time, the Franco-Prussian War (1870–1871) had a massive geopolitical impact. The French hegemony in Central Europe and Paris as the focal point of global politics was replaced by the creation of the German Empire. It also impacted the philosophical doctrine in Europe. After the war, he was a correspondent for Russia as one of the 26 founding members when the first-ever sociology society was established. We can see an evaluation of his thought process. Before Herbert Spencer's *Principles of Sociology* appeared from 1878 onwards, the French group around Emile Littré had debated some important issues. In "The Principles of Sociology" Spencer excluded the sociology of Auguste Comte's positivism, endeavouring to reformulate social science in terms of evolutionary biology. The reality is that this new science's problems and promises were discussed at meetings of the *Société de sociologie* (Heilborn, 2009).

As to Johan Heilbron's study, Auguste Comte's positive philosophy and his agenda for a new science of human society were passionately discussed in intellectual circles of Europe. Littré and his companions founded the journal *La Philosophie positive*, and their society worked to give sociology a new presence. Thus, the problems and possibilities of the new science were discussed at meetings of the Société de Sociologie, at least from 1872 to 1874. Unfortunately, little is known about those discussions. However, Roberty grew with this discussion process and came up with his thoughts on sociology.

As a member of society, de Roberty was concerned about the debate on sociology. Though politics was the dominant theme of *La Philosophie* positive, it was not a scholarly journal at all; however, we can see that a number of 20 articles on sociology were published within the period 1867–83. As a corresponding contributor, Roberty contributed seven articles together within this time (Heilborn, 2009). The most important observation from our perspective is that Roberty rejected Kantian phenomenalism and agnosticism to define sociology.

De Roberty, who was recognized as the most devoted follower of Comte, believed that Comte's positive philosophy was initially concerned with his conception of philosophy and science and its social and political implications. De Roberty hoped to expand on Comte's method in sociology by applying the descriptive method to the study of social phenomena.

In his biosocial hypothesis, de Roberty emphasized the importance of collective representations in analyzing social action. He also proposed four main factors of "supra organic" social evolution (science, philosophy, art, practical behaviour, or labour). The concept is also known as Robertism. In his study of Hecker, he outlines his "hyper positivism" in twelve theses (1915: 273–4) as below:

1) In a thorough separation of an object from the method, between two ideological species of which one precedes, engenders and fashions the other in its image;
2) In introducing, according to the empiric law of the three states, the theoretic law of correlation between the sciences and philosophy and its correlative law of the three types—or unilateral directions—of metaphysics (materialism, sensualism, idealism);
3) In demonstrating the law of identity of contrary abstractions when raised to the n th power (la loi de I'identite des contraires surabstraits); this is an equation in the world of ideas equivalent to the great law of the conservation of energy;

4) In reducing the transcendent to experience, the unknowable to the knowable, deity to the entity;
5) In reducing finality to causality;
6) In conceiving reality as an essentially homogeneous unit, be it in the elements which necessarily transform one thing into another, or be it in the laws which govern infinite evolution;
7) In distinguishing between abstract and concrete knowledge and basing the distinction upon a theory of knowledge which would complete the hierarchy of sciences established by Comte:
8) In formulating and defending the bio—sociological hypothesis in Sociology;
9) In conceiving of psychology as a concrete science of the mind made up of biological and sociological laws;
10) In conceiving of sociology as an abstract science in the world of superorganic facts, a science the essential phenomena of which are identical with the phenomena of the moral world as studied by ethics;
11) In formulating and defending the important theory which gives the order of the four great factors of superorganic evolution; these are: science, philosophy (including religion), art and work; it also specifies the principle social values, and finally indicates the conditions which sociology (or any other science) must fulfill before passing from an empiric to a theoretic state;
12) In formulating and defending a hypothesis which, departing from the present, is destined to serve the future abstract science of the superorganic world.

Hecker further noted that the ideas formulated in the above twelve theses reemerged in a revised form in his "nouveau programme de sociologie." Under three captions, Roberty further explained (1915: 274):

1. *A fundamental hypothesis of the nature of the superorganic;*
2. A scientific method;
3. *A general law of evolution.*

Here it is interesting to notice how he developed 12 theses to defend his thoughts on the development of sociology and organized them into three basic points. First, we must say it was systematic thinking carefully composed in words. Next, to merge all those 12 theses within three basic criteria, we evaluate his argument. The development of his biosocial hypothesis has been noted by the study of Efremenko and Evseeva's study (2012: 356–7) as below:

> De Roberti developed a bio-social hypothesis of the origin of society, its key category being the notion of the *super-organic*, which is a product of

the transformation of the organic form of energy into its superior form. De Roberti The super-organic is equivalent to the rational or cultured stage of the development of humankind. In the moral sphere at the pre-historic stage of development, humanity was in the state of "organic unity," i.e. biological egoism. Later, in the process of spiritual growth, man sought to pass on to the stage of the "super-organic multitude," its characteristic trait being the appearance of altruism, cooperation and solidarity. In other words, in de Roberti's conception moral behavior is an integral feature of the super-organic stage of the development of human civilization.

A critical perspective

De Roberty devoted his entire life to pursuing new knowledge in sociology and philosophy. The irony is that he was one of the most brilliant intellectuals in Russia during the pre-revolutionary period. However, he did not receive much importance and appreciation from his own country during his lifetime, and even until recently, he was a forgotten fellow.

De Roberty's areas of interest are multifaceted. He was not only a philosopher, sociologist, and critical thinker but also a human communication scholar. He underscored the need for effective communication between two or more people. He clearly said that if people communicate with each other, unite to achieve some result, and at the same time hear each other, this can accelerate the development and progress in society. But the problem is that, more often than not, we are self-interested. Accordingly, De Roberty claims a revival of humanist faith in the sociological and philosophical sciences and a belief in the possibilities of the human spirit (Kulinova Xenia, 2022).

Apart from teaching and research, he took up journalism as a profession. Though it was for a short period, not more than three years, his brilliant and dynamic journalism work made him a distinguished figure. De Roberty worked for the Saint Petersburg News, which the Russian Academy of Sciences regulated. He worked with the chief editor V. F. Korsch. The daily newspaper was the only newspaper in the then Russia where De Roberty defended liberal ideas against conservative doctrine. He continued journalism in a sensible and theoretical manner. But, as ill luck would have it, the editorial staff came under the Emperor's attack at the end of 1874. The minister of public affairs, D. A. Tolstoi, sent a secret report to the Emperor about the newspaper. De Roberty and the chief editor V. F. Korsch, were declared harmful collaborators in the confidential report. As a result, the Ministry of Public Education took complete control of the Saint Petersburg News. The entire editorial board was replaced with a new one.

He indeed began his writing on sociology as an orthodox positivist. Therefore, in his first work on sociology, he presented the definition of sociology. As he noted, "Society can and should be considered as something distinct, separate, different from biological man, as a true environment, a real external agent in relation to the isolated individual" (1893: 197). However, his ideas were not well accepted in society in the beginning. The Russian Orthodox Church condemned his early work, and de Roberti translated most of his further works into French and published them in France (Efremenko & Evseeva, 2012).

We noticed his feedback and interpretation concerning the publication of his work in Russia from the foreword that he wrote for the French edition. Worms noted his reaction in the International Journal of Sociology, which was edited by M. Giard and E. Brière from Paris (1915, Volume 23: 314):

> I would add that my book has been the object of numerous and sharp criticisms in Russia. I would be wrong to complain about them: they certainly contributed to spreading my ideas (which, in their essential foundations, are those of the positivist school) in such a part of the public which otherwise would have remained for a long time still inaccessible to them. These attacks seemed very natural to me, coming from a party where confusion of general ideas has long been on the agenda...However, I will be allowed to express one regret, that of not having been able, in the discussion raised by my book, to collect a single observation, a single objection offering the character of these useful communications that an author is always eager to make, to profit for new writing of his work.

Here are the important findings from our side: that he was aware of the state and system, and that is why he noted that the attacks seemed very natural to him as they were coming from the political party or political entity. However, he interprets such a reaction from the authority as useful communication. He notes that an author is always interested in making such communication as it benefits the writer for their new writings. He smartly applied such a positive approach in all his publications, especially since 1887, as he wrote all his French books.

This Russian scholar seconded his argument after simultaneously publishing his first work on sociology (1881) in Russian and French. His bio-social hypothesis about sociology that he conceived and followed had a tangible impact on the development of sociology as he provided the right direction. Sociologists R. Worms and D. Draghicesco acknowledged it. However, since the publication of the second edition of the book *The Past of Philosophy*, it had been censored; as a result, it appeared in French under the title *The Old and the New Philosophy*. The censorship and the accusations resulted in his prolonged exiled life in Paris (Semlali, 2005).

His career chronology reveals that he knew how to turn limitations into opportunities. Eventually facing censorship in his homeland, he continues writing in French, outside his country's land and territory, to the European Intelligentsia and academics. Eventually, we can see that in 1896 he started teaching at the New University of Brussels. In addition, he defended his position at the international congress of sociology held in Paris in 1900.

De Roberty's areas of interest were multifaceted. He was not only a philosopher, sociologist, and critical thinker but also a human communication scholar. He underscored the need for effective communication between two or more people. He clearly said that if people communicate with each other, unite to achieve some result, and at the same time hear each other, this can accelerate the development and progress in society. But the problem is that, more often than not, we are self-interested. Thus, De Roberti claims a revival of humanist faith in the sociological and philosophical sciences and a belief in the possibilities of the human spirit (Kulinova Xenia, 2022).

De Roberty explained that the importance of fruitful communication between and among people is an essential need for all individuals. People in the "pre-cultural period" (genus, tribe) were united in communities. They do not just cohabitate but also engage in joint activities and have specific goals that they strive for. This is the driving force for development: actions, behaviour, social facts, progress, scientific and technological revolution, and the emergence of previously unseen ways of mass production (Kulinova Xenia, 2022).

Conclusion

De Roberty became one of the founding fathers of Sociology at the age 35. A brilliant, bright, bold scholar and a critical thinker, De Roberty was far advanced for his time. His research allowed him to achieve great success and become a member of the International Sociological Society.

He was a man of pre-revolution Russia. His works also reflected the growing interest of Russian sociologists in issues of solidarity, altruism, and morality. His thoughts on human communication endorsed the vitality of fruitful communication, which is essential for any society's development. Unfortunately, he hasn't received much appreciation for his works in Russia to date. This chapter is an effort to shed light on De Roberty's work and life, assess his contribution to his country Russia, the western world, and the field of sociology, and expose it to international academia.

The chapter discussed his writings and books, including his "Sociological Notes" and articles. It will also reveal how the Russian authorities' censorship and sharp criticism helped him find innovative ways to express his views, such as writing in French and seeking asylum, including teaching in Paris and Brussels. However, he did not only contributed to establishing the Russian School of Higher Studies in Paris, but he also taught there for a couple of years. Finally, this chapter aims to identify whether the "Positive philosophy" moment during the time of De Roberty revealed the praxis that evolved in this academic's life until he was assassinated in 1915.

He searched for true knowledge and life values that would contribute to human society. His closest friend and colleague M. M. Kovalevsky wrote in de Roberti's obituary: "The path he paved in the field of philosophy, ethics and those that will be followed by several generations from among thinkers who refused to build these sciences on a priori principles" (1915).

References

Efremenko, D. and Evseeva, Y. 2012. Studies of social solidarity in Russia: Tradition and modern trends. *The American Sociologist, 43*(4), pp. 349–365.

Hecker, J.F. 1915. *Russian Sociology: A Contribution to the History of Sociological Thought and Theory* (Vol. 67, No. 1–2). Columbia University Press, New York.

Heilbron, J. 2009. Sociology and positivism in 19th-century France: The vicissitudes of the Société de Sociologie (1872–4). *History of the Human Sciences, 22*(4), pp. 30–62.

Kovalevsky, M. 1915 June. A Page of Our Relations with Western Philosophy (in Russian). In *The messenger of Europe*, Book 6. Saint Petersburg.

Kulinova, Xenia. 2022. *Evgeny Valentinovich De Roberti, Sociologist*. Retrived from https://spravochnick.ru/sociologiya/evgeniy_valentinovich_de_roberti_sociolog/

Lioubina, G.I. 2004. A Student of the University of Moscow in Paris. In I.L. Velikodnaia (dir.), *Rare Manuscripts and Publications* (in Russian). Indrik, Moscow, pp. 84–107.

Semlali, Y. 2005. Eugène de Roberty (1843–1915). A Little-known Page in the History of Sociology. https://halshs.archives-ouvertes.fr/halshs-00003964

Sorokin, P.A. 1927. Russian Sociology in the Twentieth Century. *American Journal of Sociology*, 31, pp. 57–69.

Sorokin, P.A. 1938. *Contemporary Sociological Theories*. Payot, Paris.

INDEX

A
Akmalova, A., 45
Andreev, F.M., 9–10
Avrich, Paul, 37

B
von Baer, Karl E., 13–15, 75
Bakunin, Mikhail, 11, 30–35, 38–39
Belinsky, V., 4
Benedict, Ruth, 91
Berelowitch, W., 111
Briere, E., 123
Brockhaus, F.A., 43, 45
Buckle, Henry Thomas, 19
Buslaev, F.I., 99

C
Carr, E.H., 32, 36
Certprof, 102, 104–105, 107–109
Chaadayev, Peter, 4
Comte, August, 15, 34, 56
Creighton, M., 91

D
Danis, M., 111
Darwin, Charles, 13, 15
Dolgova, E.A, 105–106

E
Efremenko, D., 114, 121–123
Efron, I.A., 43, 45
Evseeva, Y., 114, 121–123

G
Garibadli, J., 9
Giard, M., 123
Giryonok, F., 7
Gogol, N., 5
Gouldner, A., 38
Grigoriev, A., 3
Guillaume, James, 29
Gyuliga, A., 2

H
Heilbron, J., 120
Herzen, Alexander, 36, 43

K
Kant, Immanuel, 85, 90–91
Karaseva, T.A., 103
Kareev, N., 57–58, 99, 107, 109
Kojeve, A., 85
Konishi, S., 12–14
Korsch, V.F., 122
Korsh, V.F., 117
Kovalevsky, M., 125
Kozlova, L.A., 104
Kropotkin, Peter, 106
Kulalaeva Yu, V., 99
Kulinova, Xenia, 122, 124

L
Lavrov, P.L., 77
Lenin, V.I., 107–108
Letourneau, Charles, 19

Lileev, P., 61
Lilienfeld, Paul, 56–69
Lilienfeld-Toal, Paul, 58–64
Lioubina, G.I., 116
Lomonosov, M., 2
Losskiy, N., 6

M
Malinov A.V., 105–106
Marchenkov, V., 100–101
Masoero, A., 103, 106–107
Marx, Karl, 71
Matyushenko, G., 43
McCaffree, K., 14
Mechnikov, L., 13, 15–24
Medusheviskiy, A., 1
Mikhaylovsky, N., 70
Mochenkov, V., 108
Motroshilova, N., 83, 87, 96
Mudde, Cas, 73
Myagkov, G.P., 100, 111

N
Narodnik movements, 71–72
Narodnost, 5
Navickas, J., 89
Nemeth, T., 45, 92
Nosov, A., 2

O
Obolevitch, T., 87
Odoevsky, V., 5–6

P
Perevedentsev, E., 100–101, 110
Persona, 100
Podovoisky, D.G., 100–101, 103, 108–109
Pyziur, E., 27

R
de Roberty, Eugene, 117
Randolph, John, 28–30
Reznik, Y., 7
Rostovtsev, E.A., 101, 103, 107
Rushist, 101

S
Saharov, V., 3
Samsonova, N.G., 43

Scanlan, James P., 77–78
Schelling, 93
Semlali, Y., 115, 123
Shein, L., 93, 94
Sidorchuk, 101, 103, 107
Simons, A., 84
Sinyutin, M.V., 103, 108
Skvortsova, E.C., 102
Smerdev, I., 85
Smith, O., 84–86
Soboleva, N.A., 104
Solovyev, Vladimir S., 87–92
    Epistemic sphere, 92
    Justification of the Moral Good, 83
Sorokin, Pavel, 4
Sorokin, Pitrim A., 115
Spencer, Herbert, 14, 16, 119
Spinoza, Baruch, 85
Stankevich, N., 29
Steklov, Y., 27
Stronin, Alexander, 47–49, 51
Swiderski, E., 95
Swift, T., 100–102, 111

T
Tagore, Rabindranath, 86
Tsygarkov, D.A., 99
Turner, J.H., 14
V
Vasilev, Y., 110
Virchow, Rudolf, 65
Vuchinich, A., 1
Vvedenskiy, A., 1

W
Wagner, Richard, 36
Weber, M., 46
White, James D., 14–15
Worms, R., 56, 123
Wortman, Richard, 28

Y
Yakovenko, I., 1

Z
Zenkovsky, Vasily Vasilyevich, 92–94
Zhereb, A., 6
Zwahlen, R., 96
Zweerde, Evan der, 9

For Product Safety Concerns and Information please contact our EU
representative GPSR@taylorandfrancis.com
Taylor & Francis Verlag GmbH, Kaufingerstraße 24, 80331 München, Germany

www.ingramcontent.com/pod-product-compliance
Lightning Source LLC
Chambersburg PA
CBHW060044030426
42334CB00019B/2483

9 7 8 1 0 3 2 8 9 0 5 4 8